the happiness *diet*

Also by Rachel Kelly

Walking on Sunshine: 52 Small Steps to Happiness

Black Rainbow: How Words Healed Me—My Journey Through Depression

If: A Treasury of Poems for Almost Every Possibility (coeditor)

the happiness *diet*

Good Mood Food

Rachel Kelly

with Alice Mackintosh

Photographs by Laura Edwards

ATRIA PAPERBACK

New York   London   Toronto   Sydney   New Delhi

For Edward

ATRIA
PAPERBACK

An Imprint of Simon & Schuster, Inc.
1230 Avenue of the Americas
New York, NY 10020

Copyright © 2017 by Rachel Kelly
Photography copyright © Laura Edwards
Originally published in Great Britain in 2017 by Short Books
Published by arrangement with Short Books Limited
Previously published as *The Happy Kitchen*

First Atria Paperback edition September 2017

ATRIA PAPERBACK and colophon are trademarks of
Simon & Schuster, Inc.

For information about special discounts for bulk purchases,
please contact Simon & Schuster Special Sales at 1-866-506-1949
or business@simonandschuster.com.

The Simon & Schuster Speakers Bureau can bring authors to
your live event. For more information or to book an event, contact
the Simon & Schuster Speakers Bureau at 1-866-248-3049 or visit
our website at www.simonspeakers.com.

Interior design by Georgia Vaux

Manufactured in the United States of America

10 9 8 7 6 5 4 3 2 1

Library of Congress Cataloging-in-Publication Data

Names: Kelly, Rachel, author. | Mackintosh, Alice, author. | Edwards,
    Laura (Photographer), photographer.
Title: The happiness diet : good mood food / by Rachel Kelly with Alice
    Mackintosh ; photographs by Laura Edwards.
Description: New York : Atria Books, [2017] | Includes index.
Identifiers: LCCN 2017008690| ISBN 9781501165641 | ISBN
    9781501165665 (ebook)
Subjects: LCSH: Comfort food. | Cooking—Psychological aspects. |
    LCGFT: Cookbooks.
Classification: LCC TX714 .K448 2017 | DDC 641.3—dc23
    LC record available at https://lccn.loc.gov/2017008690

ISBN 978-1-5011-6564-1
ISBN 978-1-5011-6566-5 (ebook)

DISCLAIMER This book is based on my personal experience
of how food and the enjoyment of cooking helped me become
happier. However, it is not intended to provide medical advice, and
should not replace the guidance of a qualified physician or other
health-care professional. See your health-care provider before
making major dietary changes, especially if you have existing health
problems, medical conditions, or chronic diseases. The authors and
publishers have made every effort to ensure that the information in
this book is safe and accurate, but they cannot accept liability for
any resulting injury, loss, or damage to either property or person,
whether direct or consequential, however it arises.

I used to think of food as being physical fuel, or a way to celebrate special occasions. Now I am learning about the power of food, and its role in boosting our mental health. In recent years it has become widely accepted that we need to look after our mind in the same way that we look after our body. What is exhilarating is that changing what we eat is something we can do for ourselves.

In the field of nutrition, new research and evidence is emerging all the time, and I have done my best to report what experts are discovering. *The Happiness Diet* also reflects my personal experience and how I have become calmer and more content by changing my diet. It is intended to be a gentle guide. I don't want any rules to weigh you down. Anxiety and depression are individual experiences, and this means that the way we respond to treatment differs too.

Some of what I share in this book reflects basic biology that I wish I'd learned at school: for example, how fluctuating blood sugar affects our adrenal glands, which can trigger bouts of anxiety. Other advice addresses the effect of particular foods on our nerves, brain, and digestion, which in turn affect our moods.

There is a degree of truth to Hippocrates's claim two millennia ago that "all disease begins in the gut." Recently, scientists have advanced our understanding of the gut and its relationship with the rest of our body in fascinating ways. It is responsible for producing a large proportion of our neurotransmitters, the chemicals that communicate information throughout the body and brain. There are eight main neurotransmitters that affect our happiness, including serotonin and dopamine, sleep-inducing melatonin, and oxytocin, which is

sometimes referred to as the love hormone. In fact, as much as 90 percent of serotonin is made in our gut, and around 50 percent of dopamine. The enteric nervous system, which is the part of the nervous system embedded in our gut, contains as many neurotransmitters as our brain.

Much of the research on the links between anxiety and the health of our gut bacteria or gut microbiota has been done on mice. Indeed there are quite a few animal studies that find strong links between gut microbiota and anxiety-related behaviors. So cultivating a healthy gut may prove an important way to cheer us up. As well as supporting our immune system, a healthy gut digests vital minerals and nutrients. Without this basic function, you could eat all the Good Mood Food in the world, but still be unable to enjoy its full benefits.

Our poor, tired brain needs nourishing too. I was amazed to learn that the brain uses about one quarter of our daily energy supply, consuming around 300 calories during the day and roughly the same number at night. No other animal has quite such a hungry brain. An ape would have to eat for around 20 hours a day to feed a brain of a relative size.

I have summarized what I have learned about eating for happiness in my ten Golden Rules at the beginning of this book. These rules underpin the following chapters, in which I explain how to become more energized, more contented, less anxious, more clearheaded, more balanced, and a better sleeper by following a happy diet, and I include recipes that put the theory into practice. For me, this has led to a very happy kitchen. I hope it will make your kitchen happy too.

I have always been something of a worrier, and there have been times in the past when my anxiety has tipped me into depression. Trying to combine my working life in the newsroom of a national newspaper with the demands of a young family triggered my first major depressive episode in my thirties, which I wrote about in my memoir *Black Rainbow*.

My first breakdown was in 1997, the second in 2003. On both occasions, I was treated mainly with drugs and therapy. This book is not intended as a substitute for either medication or other strategies. Antidepressants, for example, can be a crucial recourse for those suffering from mood disorders, as indeed they were for me many years ago when I was depressed. But ideally our use of them should be short-term, as they can have adverse side effects, including, ironically, suicidal feelings and weight gain.

Because I was always hungry when taking antidepressants, I ballooned in size, which didn't help my morale. My tongue also became furred and my lips cracked. Although the side effects did lessen over time and drugs now cause fewer adverse reactions than they used to, I remember feeling desperately passive, like a powerless insect trapped in amber, unable to take any initiative to improve my own physical and mental well-being. At the time, I determined that I would find other ways to stay calm.

Gradually I managed to recover from depression, and have continued to get better over the years. I have been able to stop focusing on the heavy stuff and get on with the inevitable ups and downs of daily life. Using small, sanity-saving tools like those featured in my book *Walking on Sunshine: 52 Small Steps to Happiness* has enabled me to feel much happier, and to live more consciously.

Walking on Sunshine reflected the fact that I had already become interested in nutrition, and included a few dietary tips. Some of them were thanks to my GP. At a routine checkup to see how I was dealing with my anxiety, she told me that there was compelling evidence about the links between mood and food,

before proceeding to write down a list of "happy foods" that might keep me calm, including green leafy vegetables, dark chocolate, and oily fish.

Walking on Sunshine also has tips on meditation, a commonsense tactic that has helped to defeat my anxiety. Unsurprisingly, I had worked out the importance of regular exercise, something that many doctors agree may be at least as effective as antidepressants in treating some forms of depression. For years, poetry, too, has been a constant and helpful companion, hence the lines of poetry opening each of our chapters. For me the healing power of words complements the healing power of food. I now rely on all these approaches to staying calm and well. And following a happy diet, in particular, has become a powerful new tool in my toolbox.

I wasn't an unhealthy eater. At heart, I was a meat-and-two-veg sort of girl, not unfamiliar with more exotic ingredients like quinoa, though I didn't know how to pronounce it (keen-wa). I wasn't averse to the odd avocado, spinach, and almond milk smoothie, but was an unadventurous cook, with a few tried-and-true recipes under my belt. As my friends know, my favorite dish was fish pie and sometimes, whisper it, it was store-bought and microwavable. If anyone came for supper, it was my default: I knew that it wouldn't go wrong. Other than that, I cooked fairly basically for my family, including our dog, Sammy, who never complains when I fry a spare bit of meat or fish for him.

I had begun to change my approach to food and was struck by the difference it was making to how I felt. As I moved to a more mindful approach to cooking and eating, friends remarked that I looked well and seemed jollier. I became convinced that it was time to wind back the harm of too much medicine and prescribe a little more food, and I was eager to learn more. What else should I be eating? Were there foods I could eat for particular symptoms? What were scientists researching in the world of nutrition? Does how you cook and even how you eat make a difference to your mood? In my quest, I got chatting to doctors, therapists, cooks, psychologists, academics, dieticians, and people I have worked with when doing happiness workshops and talks for charities: I am an ambassador for the UK service organizations Sane, Rethink, and YoungMinds. Colleagues and friends shared their nutritional tips, I tried them out, and I continued to feel better.

It was time to further my knowledge and up the pace by getting the help of a nutritionist. I was getting confused with all the advice offered and felt out of my depth. Eating for happiness was proving difficult and at times bewildering. Sometimes I wished I were a rabbit, since it seemed that the only thing that was safe was lettuce.

After a bit of research I got in touch with the nutritional therapist Alice Mackintosh. At the time, she worked for a reputable nutrition clinic on London's Harley Street, advising people with all sorts of health issues. A friend had recommended her as someone interested in mood and food, and who had helped many people with anxiety.

When we met, Alice was reassuring, sympathetic, and knowledgeable—she has degrees in both nutritional therapy and biomedical science. She had intended to become a doctor, but as she learned more about nutrition, she was drawn to a career in which she could develop her knowledge of food's powerful impact on our body. I explained that I was already a believer in the importance of nutrition to my happiness, but I wanted to learn more. What else could I do when I still felt anxious? And could we work on some recipes together to make the process easier? Our resulting conversations led to this book.

With Alice's help, the supermarket microwavable fish pie was no more. Alice and I began to develop recipes for my symptoms, and she gave me practical tools in the form of meal planners. I started to keep a food diary and become even more aware of the effects different foods had on me. I even drew up a weekly planner allocating time for meals, exercise, and work. Delighted at how certain foods were

helping with my symptoms, I started to formulate some golden rules for happier eating, and the more I followed them, the better I felt.

Over time, I also gained confidence as a cook. I tried Alice's recipes, which were designed for a kitchen novice rather than a chef. I experimented with the ingredients she suggested, and learned to cook with globe-trotting tahini and harissa paste, lemongrass and cilantro. There was no pressure to perform, just to find my feet in the kitchen.

I realized a joyful kitchen could calm me as much as the food itself. Cooking reawakened my jaded senses, connecting me with nature in a way similar to gardening, something I have always found soothing. The hiss of peppers sizzling in a pan, the scent of ginger and garlic, the sight of rich reds and yellows: all this could, I realized, gladden my soul.

As I know all too well from my own experience with anxiety, cooking is not always top of the agenda. When I was still feeling low, I found the best way to make progress was to take small steps and tackle one symptom at a time. That is why each chapter in this book offers recipes and meal plans designed to target a particular symptom, so you can turn straight to the one you need. These recipes are not just tasty but manageable. Many of them involve putting a few things in a blender. There's also a quick recipe in each chapter for those times when you feel unable to cook much—our Feeling Fragile recipes.

We have aimed to use affordable, readily available ingredients as much as possible. Where relevant, we have also included seasonal, cheaper options. Surveys show that many of the people most in need of the nutrients we refer to are those on low incomes. These people also face the challenge of tempting deals on food with a lower nutritional value.

Making the right decisions in the supermarket or health food store is crucial to your quest to eat more happily. Our **Good Mood Food Index** at the back of the book will help you shop with your mood in mind. This index, in which foodstuffs are listed in order from Fab Mood Foods to Low Mood Foods, was devised for me by Alice as a helpful aid in my own journey toward harnessing the power of food to feel more cheerful. Think of it as a handy reminder, something to stick on your fridge and consult when you're short of time. There's also a second list of foods divided by season, another handy guide to have in your bag when you go shopping.

I didn't just change *what* I ate. I also changed my relationship with food, from the process of cooking to how I consumed it. Thanks to a mindfulness course, I began to eat in a slower, more attentive way—see our section on **Mindful Eating** on page 184.

Today, cooking is an important part of what keeps me sane. I am reassured by its rituals: weighing out the ingredients, chopping the vegetables, whisking, beating, folding, slicing, assembling, not to mention the joy of indulging in the end results. Perhaps I am imagining this, but I have even noticed that those who come for dinner leave in a lighter mood than before. Maybe that's because I am better company than I used to be, or they're relieved not to be eating fish pie again. I used to feel I was both a boring and a bored cook, buying the same ingredients for the same recipes. My kitchen is now a place of creativity and adventure, although I've had to learn the hard way which recipes work, which don't, and which taste awful.

It hasn't always been an easy journey. In addition to Alice's companionship and support, a number of approaches have helped. The first was to include plenty of treats to reward my progress. Using rewards is a proven method of helping to change our lifestyle habits. The nibbles featured in the **Comfort Food** chapter of this book taste better than the store-bought doughnuts or cookies I used to turn to when feeling low. Importantly, they lift my mood, rather than hinder it. They are some of my favorite things to make.

Accepting the power of compromise has also been important. If I have a cooked breakfast, I'll add tomatoes, herbs, and mushrooms, and no longer eat sausages. Instead of cereal, I have oatmeal, and I use fruit to sweeten plain yogurt rather than buying flavored containers.

In addition, my family has helped me eat more happily. I live in London with my husband, Sebastian, and have three sons and two daughters, ranging in age from 13 to 22. My family doesn't always use the same recipes I do, but they have been involved in my culinary journey, and we have enjoyed making the dishes together.

In particular, I wanted to cook with my children alongside me, something I was fortunate to experience when I was a child, watching my mother chop an onion, or painting a glaze of apricot jam on one of her apple tarts. Hitherto I had rarely done the same with my own children, apart from making the odd cake. Instilling in them the value of Good Mood Food as they set up their own kitchens has been hugely helpful to me in return.

It is a commonplace that trying to benefit others helps us. Though I could find no psychological research to prove it, I have found that one of my most reliable routes to personal happiness is to cook for others. But I have also learned to savor eating on my own. Whereas I would once eat standing with the fridge door yawning, I now set a place, even if it is for one. Using china and a place mat makes a difference to how sunny I feel when I am eating, in much the same way that beer, for some, tastes better in a bottle than in a can.

The appearance of the dish makes a difference too. Many of our recipes are designed to look pretty on the plate. They're not just pretty, though; they work. Following the **Golden Rules**, the recipes, and my other well-established strategies has enabled me to regain the peace of mind that my illness once stripped away. Like anyone, I still feel anxious on occasion, but I am happy and well and have a busy life working alongside charities and as a journalist and writer on well-being. Meanwhile, Alice now runs a thriving nutrition practice of her own.

Let's get started!

Rachel (right) with nutritional therapist Alice Mackintosh.

1. Eat mostly plants

Like many of you, no doubt, I had often heard this advice. The links between our health and eating a plant-based diet have been outlined in numerous studies: physically, such diets have been associated with a decreased risk of heart disease and some cancers. What I didn't realize is how much the positive cycle between the physical and mental means that such a diet could benefit our psychological health too.

One reason a plant-based diet is so important is that our brain and digestive system are still adapting to our changing environment. Our hunter-gatherer ancestors ate a large variety of whole, unrefined plants. Huge changes to the human diet over the past 200 years may have run ahead of our ability to adapt. Our modern diet of processed and refined foods is different from the one that, for most of our evolutionary history, we have thrived on. The downside of this new way of life is reflected in soaring obesity rates and physical illnesses such as type 2 diabetes, which in turn can exacerbate anxiety and depression.

A second reason that plants are so important is related to an enzyme—called MAO—which is thought to break down beneficial hormones such as serotonin. Fruits and vegetables may help stop this enzyme working. Read our **Nutrition Note** on page 14 for more details on this.

A final theory is that plants may contribute to our mood because they contain antioxidants that "mop up" or neutralize supposedly dangerous free radicals. These fun-sounding compounds are unstable molecules that can, in excess, damage tissues and vital cell structures. They may play an important role in the development of depression, potentially causing the death of nerve cells in certain emotional areas of the brain. Another more recent view is that the body has its own mechanisms in place to control the balance of these free radicals. While the exact role of antioxidants is uncertain and more complex than we previously thought, types such as beta-carotene, flavonoids, selenium, and vitamins A, C, and E, are all health-enhancing.

Yet despite the many benefits of eating plants, only one-third of adults in the UK consume the recommended five portions of fruit and vegetables each day—and in the US the proportion is slightly less. Many think that this recommendation should be increased to seven. Which is what I try to do—with the emphasis on the vegetables, since although fresh fruit is good for you, it contains quite a lot of sugar, and too much of the more sugary sorts (particularly tropical fruits such as pineapple and mango) can increase blood sugar levels. The more plants I eat, the happier I feel.

To ensure I get my daily fix, I divide my main course plate at lunch and dinner as follows: half vegetables, a quarter whole-grain carbohydrates, and a quarter protein. A plate following this formula will by default normally also contain most of the fats you need, whether in the form of an olive oil dressing or in the oily fish or nuts or other protein sources you choose. I also try to make sure I eat a rainbow of colored vegetables, to ensure I get the full range of phytonutrients. Remembering rainbows is an easy way to remember what to eat.

2. Use herbs and spices

This Golden Rule sits next to the need to eat mostly plants. Herbs and spices are my friends because cooking with them has helped me to up the amount of vegetables I eat, as they add natural and enticing flavors. I used to think of vegetables as a side rather than a main dish, but now that I know how to make them delicious, they take pride of place. As well as being tasty, some herbs and spices may trigger digestive processes that can help the body benefit from meals.

We have used both saffron and turmeric, a bright yellow root found in Indian cooking, in a lot of our recipes, as they may help alleviate depression.

Saffron has been used in healing for thousands of years; it was first mentioned as a medicine in the ancient Greek city of Thera. And scientists have recently concluded that it might be an option in the

treatment of low mood: when compared to Prozac, it was found to have a similar effect on symptoms. We still have a long way to go before these findings can be confirmed, and larger-scale trials need to be carried out before anyone replaces their pills with this most vibrant of spices. But I love it. Saffron is expensive, so cook with as much as you can afford. If nothing else, the scent of it can be soothing: another small study found that its aroma had some beneficial effects on symptoms associated with menstruation.

3. Go to seed

Sprinkling seeds on everything from soups to salads has been another useful way of making vegetables more appealing. Now and then I toast a selection of sunflower, pumpkin, butternut squash, and any other seeds and pop them in a jar ready to be used. Seeds are the eggs of the plant world. They contain all the genetic instructions and nutrients to produce life. These include magnesium, B vitamins, selenium, and calcium, along with protein and healthy fats. Some seeds are also a source of tryptophan, the amino acid that is the building block of serotonin. We cannot make tryptophan ourselves, so we have to get it from our diets, a recurring theme in this book. Seeds are a plant source, so find your inner squirrel. We advise sticking to around two portions a day.

4. Eat for your gut, "the second brain"

The gut or gastrointestinal tract is the long tube that starts at our mouth and ends at our back passage. It is controlled by the autonomous nervous system, which also controls our breathing, body temperature, and blood pressure, acting mostly without our conscious effort. Consequently, Michael Gershon, professor of pathology and cell biology at Columbia University in New York, has referred to this extraordinary system as "the second brain." I was riveted when I learned that it is not solely our brain that controls our body. No wonder we talk about "gut feelings."

Not only is the gut home to 90 percent of our serotonin, as mentioned in the introduction, it is also one of the first lines of defense against bacteria and viruses. The lining of the intestine acts as a barrier, allowing nutrients to pass through but preventing most large molecules and germs from getting into the bloodstream. If we are stressed, our digestive system may work ineffectively and even become inflamed. This in turn may affect our mood.

To feel calm, we need to nourish our guts by encouraging healthy bacteria to flourish, and so help avoid inflammation. Our **Nice and Calm** chapter gives details about how to nourish a healthy gut, but in summary, we should avoid resorting to antibiotics unless absolutely needed, as well as alcohol, fatty cuts of meat, gluten, burned food, and processed foods, and eat more anti-inflammatory omega-3s, herbs, spices, and colorful fruits and vegetables.

Nutrition Note: why eating vegetables helps—the role of enzymes
Several studies have found a correlation between diets high in vegetables, fruits, meats, and whole grains and lower levels of depressive and anxiety disorders, when compared to a Western diet high in red meat, sugary desserts, high-fat foods, and refined grains (sometimes dubbed the "meat-sweet" diet). A 2012 study of elderly Taiwanese men and women found that more frequent consumption of vegetables was associated with reduced depressive symptoms. The reasons why eating fruit and vegetables might impact mental health are wide-ranging, but one might involve their capacity to inhibit an enzyme called monoamine oxidase, or MAO, which can break down both serotonin and dopamine. Fruits and vegetables high in phytonutrients, such as apples, berries, grapes, and onions, may help to regulate MAO activity. This means that, in turn, fewer beneficial neurotransmitters get broken down, and hence we may feel better.

5. Fats are my friends, and remember number 3

Our brain is made up of about 60 percent fat. I have never seen a brain, but I am told it looks rather like a pat of pale butter. So the brain needs some fats, and it is important to consume the right types. The main fats to remember are the omegas. These healthy fats are named after the last letter of the Greek alphabet: they contain a long chain of carbon atoms, with one end referred to as the alpha end, and the other the omega end. There are three main types of omegas—omega-3s, omega-6s, and omega-9s—with omega-3s being the most important to a happy diet and the lucky number to remember. As you will see in our **Nutrition Note** below, there's evidence that omega-3s can improve our mood.

I now eat oily fish, algae known as spirulina, walnuts, and various seeds to boost my omega-3 supplies, and we have lots of recipes with these ingredients so you can do the same. While prioritizing omega-3, we do need some omega-6s and omega-9s. I aim for healthier, less processed forms from avocado, nuts, seeds, and sesame and rapeseed oil.

Dairy products also contain important nutrients for our health, and I haven't found it necessary, as is fashionable, to eliminate them completely. Our Happiness Diet is about balance: I have reduced my intake of foods that are high in saturated fat such as fatty meats, cream, hard cheese, and, I'm afraid, my beloved pork rinds because, while scientists are researching the precise links between saturated fats and cholesterol, what is clear is that too much saturated fat is not good for our hearts. However, eggs and—hooray!—dairy products, including butter and milk, as well as the fats in moderate amounts of unprocessed meat, nurture our brain, while the microbes found in natural yogurt contribute to the diversity of our gut flora.

How much is a moderate amount? A rough rule is two portions a day. Animal products, including pork, chicken, and full-fat dairy products, contain arachidonic acid, which is a potentially inflammatory compound. Some arachidonic acid is beneficial, particularly in the development of the brain and nervous system in fetuses and infants. But, as is so often the nutritional case, we need this acid in moderation—too much of this type of animal fat may contribute to low mood, one more reason why researchers think those on more plant-based diets seem to be more cheerful.

Meanwhile, I do my best to avoid trans fats. Trans fats are different from saturated fats and no one has a good word to say about them. While trans fats can be found naturally at low levels in some foods, such as meat and dairy products, most are man-made. They are created when vegetable oils are converted into solid or semisolid fats in a process called hydrogenation. Cookie, cake, and fast-food manufacturers love hydrogenation because it stops food from going rancid, but such has been the outcry against trans fats recently that many food manufacturers have removed them from their products. Keep an eye out for any labels that still display the dread words "contains partially

Nutrition Note: omega-3s

Omega-3s appear to be the most crucial fatty acids for our brain. There are two main types, both of which we have to get from our diets: eicosapentaenoic acid (EPA) and docosahexaenoic acid (DHA). EPA makes neurotransmitters, enabling them to be detected by our cell membranes, whereas DHA is an important part of the cell-building process.

Both work to reduce inflammatory reactions. And combined evidence from a number of recent studies found that, in general, omega-3s were effective in improving depressive symptoms in both patients diagnosed with major depression and depressed patients whose symptoms did not result in a clinical diagnosis.

hydrogenated fat or oil." However difficult it might be to turn down that cake or resist that convenience meal, it is worth it since some studies have shown a link between intake of trans fats and the risk of depression.

6. Get the right balance of protein—and fish should be at the top of your list

We are omnivores, with teeth, jawbones, and a digestive system that are different from those of fruit-eating monkeys, for example. Meat, fish, eggs, and dairy provide many important nutrients such as zinc, iron, B vitamins, and iodine. I found that whenever I abandoned meat and fish during bouts of vegetarianism, I had to work doubly hard to ensure that I consumed enough of these nutrients.

As a general rule, I make sure a quarter of my plate is protein, as previously mentioned. Variety is good, and you can choose from the above foods, or vegetable sources such as beans, lentils, or seeds, but you will need to eat more of these, as they have a lower protein content. Some livestock are given antibiotics and other medication, so it is worth buying organic meat if you can afford it. In addition, grass-fed is better than grain-fed meat, as it is thought to contain more nutrients and more balanced and healthier fat.

But if you have a choice, go for fish, ideally oily fish. It is a source of our friends the omega-3s as well as many other nutrients. All fish, though, is good. Find out more in our **Nutrition Note** below.

I know there are concerns that oily fish can be contaminated with toxic chemicals called dioxins, as well as mercury, which is certainly nasty stuff and can impact our moods and the fragile architecture of our brain, as well as our cardiovascular system.

According to the World Health Organization, mercury may have a negative effect on the nervous, digestive, and immune systems, as well as the lungs, kidneys, skin, and eyes. It can impair our concentration and our memory, and should be avoided by pregnant women because it can also be damaging to fetuses.

The most common sources of mercury are cigarette smoke, preservatives, dental amalgam, and car emissions. It is also present in some fish and dairy products, as well as corn and wheat. For this reason, it is recommended that we eat no more than four portions of oily fish a week. There are no limits regarding white fish, except for sea bream, sea bass, halibut, and turbot, which should be treated as oily fish.

The older and bigger the fish, the higher the mercury content, so you may wish to choose smaller oily fish such as anchovies, herring, and salmon over larger varieties such as tuna and swordfish, which tend to accumulate more mercury, as they live longer. That said, and while no one would advocate eating something that is dangerous, some scientists are now arguing that the dangers of mercury in fish have been exaggerated. They point to the longevity of children born to Japanese women who consumed large amounts of seafood. They also highlight the huge benefits seafood brings. In view of this, and given how important oily fish is to our happiness, I cannot resist offering here a full list: anchovies, carp, herring (plus kipper and hilsa), jack mackerel (also known as scad, horse mackerel, and trevally), pilchards, salmon, sardines, trout, tuna, and whitebait.

Nutrition Note: fish
A study in Finland in 2001 found that a higher fish consumption was associated with a lower incidence of depressive symptoms. However, the study reflected correlation rather than causation: that is, the types of people who eat fish are less likely to experience depressive symptoms, but the differences could be due to their affluence, education, or awareness of fish's health benefits. A second study from New Zealand in 2002 found that fish consumption was associated with "higher self-reported mental health status"—an individual's personal perception of his or her mood, outlook, and depression scores.

7. Avoid sweeteners and additives

There has been much debate over the years about the effects of aspartame, an artificial sweetener often found in soft drinks and processed and "diet" foods. Some organizations, such as the European Food Safety Authority (EFSA), consider it safe for consumption; however, there is some evidence that it has a negative effect on mood.

Look out for additives such as aspartame and MSG on food labels—as they can be hidden in the most unexpected of places (cereals, jams, and "nutrition bars," to name but a few).

It has been helpful for me to keep a food diary, which enables me to track the decisions I am making, and alerts me to any potentially less healthy habits, such as the occasional diet cola. I have found that cutting down on soft drinks not only benefits my teeth but can also stop me from feeling jittery, as many of them contain large amounts of caffeine and sugar.

A note, too, on salt: many of us consume more salt than is good for us, so we have left it out of our recipes. Of course, feel free to season with salt and pepper as you see fit.

8. Keep an eye on blood sugar levels

As a quick Golden Rule—I will be returning to this topic in our first chapter—the steadier your blood sugar levels, the more stable and balanced you will feel. Cutting out added sugar, combining protein with unrefined carbohydrates, and not snacking are all useful habits I have adopted in order to improve my mood. While the occasional healthy snack can help to keep my blood sugar steady, there is now quite a well-rehearsed argument against grazing through the day and plenty of evidence that keeping fasting windows between meals helps fight type 2 diabetes. I have found that adding a bit of protein to something sugary like dried fruit is a handy way of managing my blood sugar, although I do not want to give the impression that adding protein makes too much sugar acceptable. There is always the same amount of sugar in dried fruit whatever you eat it with.

9. Vary your diet

This rule is one of my favorites. Eating a wide variety of foods makes for a merry diet. Once you become more aware of what you have been eating, you'll probably begin to notice that the same foods come up routinely. That was certainly the case for me—yes, eating that fish pie again and again. Adding new ingredients not only introduces a new element to your cooking, but is both physically and mentally beneficial. Foods work better combined than in isolation, which is why the notion of single "super foods" can be misleading.

Simple tricks I use to add variety include always trying to order something different if I am lucky enough to be eating out, and finding the confidence to experiment with recipes and ingredients at home rather than rolling out the same dish. (You know what it is by now.) Feel free to be as imaginative as you want with our recipes. Throw in some other ingredients, or add a few of your personal favorites. We'd love to hear about what you've been inspired to

Nutrition Note: aspartame

Aspartame contains phenylalanine, an amino acid that we need only in moderation. It is thought that it may hinder the production of serotonin, which can make some people feel flat. Meanwhile, there has also been research into how artificial sweeteners like saccharin might change our intestinal bacteria in an unhelpful way.

In an experiment in the United States in 2014, healthy individuals were split into two groups. Half were given a higher dose of aspartame. The other half received a lower dose. Then the groups swapped. After only eight days, those on the higher dose showed more signs of depression and irritability and performed worse on certain brain tests.

create. You'll find details about how to join the Happiness Diet conversation on social media at the end of this book. Eating what's in season is another good way to achieve a more varied diet. Sadly, the idea of a friendly neighborhood greengrocer who will recommend what's in season is from yesteryear, hence our guide at the end of the book.

10. Relax and enjoy

This most important of rules isn't a rule at all. When I was feeling low, I was unable to appreciate the pleasure of preparing, cooking, and eating food. As I have recovered, I have been able to rid myself of damaging old habits and now find the whole process hugely enjoyable—but it has taken time and I have had lots of help.

Be kind to yourself. While I'd like to stick to my Golden Rules all the time, sometimes it is difficult. I aim for an 80:20 balance: most of the time I eat nutritiously, but I allow myself a few treats here and there, and they are treats that I eat consciously and with enjoyment rather than with guilt. Eating less healthily is less damaging than beating yourself up about it, a habit I used to have. Eating more slowly and consciously is at the heart of my happy kitchen. I always used to finish meals first in our family and hardly noticed what I had eaten. Adopting a more mindful approach means I now enjoy the pleasures of the table. Head to the back of this book to learn more about how mindfulness helped me relax and enjoy my food.

From "Keep Right on to the End of the Road"

Keep right on to the end of the road,
Keep right on to the end,
Tho' the way be long,
Let your heart be strong,
Keep right on round the bend.

Sir Harry Lauder

balanced energy

Fatigue can be one of the most potent side effects of antidepressants. At the height of my depressive episodes, I would wake up feeling exhausted and spend the rest of the day longing for the moment when I could crawl back into bed. I used to recite the traditional Scottish song "Keep Right on to the End of the Road" on my worst days . . . if it worked for Birmingham City soccer fans, it could work for me.

When I met Alice, I was no longer exhausted in the same way. But like anyone managing a busy life, I was often tired. There were days when I struggled to find the energy to cook properly or have regular meals. The effort was too much.

Working on a routine
Of course I would love to feel perkier, I told Alice. But shouldn't we deal with my anxiety first? Actually, she explained, it made more sense to boost my energy levels before we addressed feeling anxious. Once I felt more energetic, I would in turn exercise more and sleep better.

The best way to change was to establish a routine, planning when I would wake up and go to sleep, how much exercise I would do, and when I would work, as much as when and what I would eat. Our body appreciates routine, and of all the steps I have taken to eat more happily, this is among the most important.

I was struck by how planning my meals and my days made me feel better, because it felt like I was taking control. When we eat doesn't work in isolation from everything else we do. By boosting my energy levels through regular meals, I found that, as Alice predicted, I had more strength to exercise, which in turn boosted my energy levels. A day when I ate regularly and exercised was a day on which I tended to sleep well.

While I now find cooking fun, it is a habit that at first I needed to reinforce, otherwise on some days even the prospect of warming up some soup could seem insurmountable. Alice's support and my timetable were steps toward finding the self-discipline to cook regularly. I printed out copies of my timetable and stuck them to my bathroom mirror and other places around the house to remind myself of what I was trying to achieve. To begin with, the changes were about me. Gradually they became about the whole family.

Balancing blood sugar
Having planned when I would eat, the next step was what to eat. Balancing my blood sugar was the principle I needed to adopt to become more energetic. I got to grips with the glycemic index (GI).

("Glycemic" refers to the presence of sugar in the blood.)

The GI ranks foods based on the speed at which they boost our blood sugar after we eat them, from 1 to 100, with 100 being pure sugar. White refined carbohydrates, as found in white bread, pasta, and rice, have a higher GI. Their whole-grain counterparts, such as rye bread, spelt pasta, and brown rice, all have a lower GI due to their high fiber content. This means they release sugar more slowly into the bloodstream, preventing the sharp fluctuations in blood sugar that can make us tired and jittery. For this reason, we use whole grains throughout this book. Try our *Satisfying Shrimp Penne with Broccoli*. Other foods that are rich in fiber include chickpeas, sweet potatoes, and avocados. See our recipe for *Spelt and Spinach Crepes with Avocado*, a recipe I am particularly fond of since it is one of the first I made under my new regime. Gosh, I felt proud when I served up the pancakes to my family for the first time.

I also became mindful of a food's glycemic load (GL). This is a second index that provides a more thorough picture of what particular combinations of foods will do to your blood sugar. So, for example, a watermelon is high in sugar and scores high on the GI. But because there's so little carbohydrate bulk in a watermelon, with most of it being water, it has a lower GL score. GL is calculated by multiplying the grams of available carbohydrate in a food by its GI.

You don't need to know the GI or GL for all foods by heart. I certainly don't. But having an idea of how much sugar and fiber something contains is useful, as is understanding that combining carbohydrate-rich foods with protein can reduce the GL of a meal.

What I do know is that a slow, steady release of energy improves my mood. When blood sugar levels dip below normal, stress hormones are released, which unlock the body's glucose store to give us energy. Though we can rely on this mechanism in an emergency, excess stress hormones such as adrenaline and cortisol can heighten anxiety. Their effects include a rapid heartbeat, a racing mind, nervousness, sleeplessness, and quickened breathing.

Dramatic fluctuations in these hormones may therefore lead to correspondingly dramatic swings in mood.

Being careful about how much sugar I consume not only helps me feel calm, it also lowers my risk of diabetes, which could be linked to depression. Current research suggests that the prevalence of depression could be up to three times greater in patients with type 1 diabetes and twice as high in patients with type 2 diabetes when compared to people without diabetes. The relationship between diabetes and depression is still not fully understood, however, and scientists from King's College London are now investigating possible genetic links between the two, and attempting to develop treatments that could simultaneously help both.

Breakfast is important for ensuring my energy levels, although whether breakfast is necessary for everyone is debated. Some of the evidence promoting it comes from breakfast cereal companies, and many of the most energetic people I know don't eat breakfast. Other research suggests breakfast may help stabilize mood and improve concentration in children. My breakfasts now usually consist of foods that are high in protein or complex carbohydrates, such as oats and seeds. Try our *Nutritiously Nutty Granola*. Eating breakfasts like this coupled with fruits that are lower in sugar, such as berries, kiwis, or pears, rather than the intensely sweet melons, grapes, mango, and banana, sets me up for a productive day. Swapping my usual coffee at the breakfast table for a *Tropical Vitamin C Smoothie* helps to energize me too.

If you have a sweet tooth like me, try to find natural sweetness in fruits, nuts, and spices such as cinnamon, which I have learned to sprinkle with moderate abandon; read our **Nutrition Note** on page 25 for more information. It has been too hard and joyless for me to give up sugar completely. But I have reduced how much I eat by cutting it out for two weeks. It was hard, but after that I had less of a sweet tooth and was more aware how sugary a food could be. Even a grape seems madly sweet if you've avoided sugar for a few weeks.

Chromium may reduce sugar cravings too. Chromium is a metallic element that we all require in very small amounts; it plays an essential part in the metabolic processes that regulate blood sugar, and helps insulin transport glucose into cells where it can be used for energy. See our **Essential Foods** section (page 44) for chromium-rich foods, and our **Comfort Food** chapter for some more healthy, sweet snacks that now give me the equivalent sense of reward that I once experienced from sugar. You will find more information about the importance of chromium in that chapter.

Through the day I now swap out quick-release sugars for slow ones, use brown rice instead of white, and choose fiber-rich foods such as kale and broccoli, which provide a steady release of energy. I snack on protein like almonds and cottage cheese. *Walnut and Arugula Pesto with Edamame* and *Sweet Roasted Chinese Cashews* are particularly good if you are whacked and don't feel up to much cooking.

Iron

Iron is fundamental to our energy levels. It is essential for keeping our blood oxygenated, and a deficiency can leave you feeling fatigued. A blood test revealed that I was iron-deficient, and I recommend that you get yourself tested if you are TATT—the doctor's acronym for Tired All the Time.

The best sources of iron include red meat, so try our *Iron-Rich Steak Salad*. Dark, leafy vegetables such as kale and watercress, legumes, edamame, and dried fruits also boost our iron levels—you don't need to have a steak for breakfast. Because vitamin C aids the absorption of iron, I consume iron-rich foods with a glass of orange juice or a satsuma—or our *Tropical Vitamin C Smoothie*.

Now, armed with all these strategies, in the words that opened this chapter, onward I go, right on to the end of the road.

Summing up—to become more energized, I:

established a routine

balanced my blood sugar

increased the amount of iron in my diet

Nutrition Note: cinnamon for blood sugar balance
Cinnamon's impact on blood glucose and insulin levels has been the subject of much discussion, not least because of its potential impact on relieving the symptoms of type 2 diabetes, which is now a significant worldwide problem. It is estimated that by 2025, five million people will have diabetes in the UK—and the number is higher in the US. As mentioned previously, there may be a link between chronic illnesses such as diabetes and depressive and anxiety disorders.

A number of animal and clinical research studies have indicated that cinnamon has positive effects on mice (genetically modified to mimic diabetic humans): their insulin sensitivity was improved, and the impact of stress on their brain cells was reduced. This could mean that cinnamon can boost brainpower and concentration. The weight of evidence does seem to point toward the use of moderate amounts of cinnamon in cooking as a general support for blood sugar balance. But it is important to state that it should not be used as a substitute for medication for patients diagnosed with diabetes.

TROPICAL VITAMIN C SMOOTHIE

I have this smoothie for breakfast if I wake feeling whacked. Alice designed it so that I could get lots of energy-boosting goodness in one go. If you can't find papaya, use fresh mango or pineapple. These fruits are rich in vitamin C and fiber (this is a good drink to have with iron-rich foods since the vitamin C aids the iron's absorption), while the walnuts and avocado deliver protein and healthy fats to balance everything out. The oats and nuts add substance and slow down the absorption of sugar from the fruit. The cinnamon may also reduce sugar cravings. Depending on your preference, you can add slightly more or less almond milk. Store-bought almond milk is fortified with vitamins and minerals, but also tends to have added sugar. If you want to make your own, see our recipe on page 122. Our milk has a creamy texture and a delicious nutty taste. Cow's milk also contains plenty of nutrients and, not being lactose-intolerant, I sometimes use it in smoothies.

– Serves 2 –

½ papaya or 1 whole mango
¼ avocado
1 Tablespoon rolled oats
6 walnuts
1 cup almond, coconut, or oat milk, or
   use organic low-fat cow's milk
Cinnamon to taste

1. Peel the papaya or mango and remove its seeds or pit.

2. Chop it into medium-size chunks and pop it into the blender with all the other ingredients. Blend until smooth.

NUTRITIOUSLY NUTTY GRANOLA

Both Alice and I had made lots of different granolas over the years, but this is the best so far. Its nuts and seeds make it a source of omega-3s, omega-6s, and omega-9s, and the oats provide me with a slow release of steady energy.

The exotic goji berries add color and intensity of flavor. They are bright red and hail from China and the Himalayas. They are also known as wolfberries, and have been used to treat a host of ailments for centuries as part of traditional Chinese medicine. I enjoy their tartness and scarlet hue, which peps up all the browns in our granola.

Coconut oil has a delicate flavor; it is solid at room temperature and needs to be melted, which is why we use it for cooking. While it has been rather fashionable of late, we use it more for its flavor than its health benefits. It contains 90 percent saturated fat, a higher percentage than butter. Though saturated fats are not the heart-clogging villains they were once thought to be, and there is even some research (though only from a short-term study) to suggest coconut oil might increase "good" HDL cholesterol, it's best to consume it in moderation and make sure it is not the only oil you use. I use olive oil more often, as it both lowers LDL ("bad") cholesterol and increases HDL cholesterol.

I have made this recipe many times, and have learned a few things. First, remember to take the pan off the heat before adding the coconut oil and maple syrup; if you leave it on, it all gets a bit too fudgy, which, though delicious, makes it difficult to mix with the dry ingredients. If you want the recipe to go further, add a few more oats, but be sure to add more liquid if you do so. Avoid extra-thick oats, which soak up more moisture and can make the mixture too dry. I like to make my granola in advance, and it tends to last for a few weeks, but feel free to halve the quantities if you want less.

continued on next page

4 ounces Brazil nuts
4 ounces pecans
2 cups rolled oats
4 ounces sliced almonds
4 ounces sunflower seeds
4 ounces pumpkin seeds
3 ounces shredded coconut or
  unsweetened dried coconut
4 ounces hard dates
½ cup water
2 teaspoons ground cinnamon
1 teaspoon pure vanilla extract
3–4 Tablespoons liquid coconut oil
3–4 Tablespoons maple syrup
2 ounces goji berries

1. Preheat the oven to 350°F.

2. Roughly chop the Brazil nuts and pecans by hand into ⅛-inch chunks. You can chop them in a food processor but they will break up into powder quickly, so be careful.

3. Put the oats, all the nuts and seeds, and the coconut flakes in a large bowl.

4. Chop the dates into quarters and put them in a small pan with around ½ cup water. Gently simmer on the stove for 2–5 minutes or until they soften. Take them off the heat, and then add the coconut oil, maple syrup, cinnamon, and vanilla. It should form a lovely, sticky, gooey mixture with pieces of soft date still visible.

5. Combine the two mixtures and stir, evenly distributing the brown syrup throughout. It should be relatively soft but not wet. Add more coconut oil if it feels too dry.

6. Spread the mixture over two large baking sheets and bake in the oven for 20 minutes, stirring twice during cooking to make sure the top doesn't burn. It should be crunchy and golden, but not too dark.

7. Take the baking sheets out of the oven and scatter the goji berries on top so that they soften slightly. Let the granola cool.

8. Once the granola is cool, store it in an airtight container in the fridge. It will keep for up to 2 months.

ALMOND AND TOASTED PECAN SPREAD

This spread is best stored in jars, and should keep for around 2 months. Spread it on toast or oatcakes, or add to smoothies, yogurt, or fruit. It can also serve as a cheesecake or banoffee base. My children like it as part of a packed lunch: the protein from the nuts keeps them going throughout the fast-paced school day. What's more, it is rich in choline, which plays a role in a number of bodily processes, particularly nerve function. You will find more about choline in our *Mental Clarity* chapter.

– Serves 15–20 –

4 ounces pecans
7 ounces raw whole almonds, ideally soaked
   overnight in water. You can either use
   blanched almonds or ones with skin,
   which will alter the color of the finished
   result. (Blanched almonds undergo a brief
   heating process, which removes the skin.)
1 Tablespoon liquid coconut oil
1 teaspoon ground cinnamon
5 pitted dates (optional)
1 Tablespoon maple syrup or honey

1. Lightly toast the pecans in a pan for 2–3 minutes, tossing them regularly to prevent them from burning. Let them cool for 15 minutes.

2. Drain the almonds, place them in a food processor, and blend for 3–5 minutes, or until they start to form a slightly wet powder. Stop and stir every minute or so to check the consistency, which can vary depending on the machine you are using.

3. Put the coconut oil, pecans, and cinnamon into the processor and continue to blend until a paste is formed. This should take another 3–5 minutes. You can add dates at this stage; the end result will take on a more fudgy consistency. You may need to stop the machine and scrape down the sides a few times.

4. If you haven't used dates, taste the mixture and add a little maple syrup or honey if you want it sweeter. You could add a teaspoon more of coconut oil if you feel the mixture needs to be loosened a little. Blend for another 2–3 minutes for a smoother result, scraping down the sides of the food processor periodically.

SPELT AND SPINACH CREPES WITH AVOCADO

These crepes will always have a special place in my heart because I had such a sense of achievement the first time I made them. My kitchen felt very happy indeed. They take about 15 minutes to make, so they're great if you are starving and want something quick and fresh for lunch or a light dinner. Spinach is a source of iron— remember Popeye. Spelt provides steady energy and, though once a rarity, is now widely stocked in supermarkets. Other whole-grain flours work well too. This recipe is filling, and keeps you going all morning.

I like the green crepe effect, but you don't have to add the spinach to the batter. If you prefer, you can pop it inside the crepe at the end with the avocado and smoked salmon. Spice up the filling by adding whatever takes your fancy. I am a fan of wasabi, an elusive Japanese root that grows next to highland mountain streams. It takes two years to reach maturity and is quite perishable, and therefore expensive to ship. So most of the wasabi paste you buy is in fact based on our more homespun horseradish. Either way, the stuff clears your sinuses in the same way that mustard and horseradish do.

– Serves 2 –

¾ cup plus 2 Tablespoons whole-grain flour,
  such as spelt, buckwheat, or brown rice
2 eggs
2 ounces spinach leaves
1¼ cups cow's milk or a dairy-free option—
  unsweetened almond milk works well
½ teaspoon wasabi (optional)
4 teaspoons oil
1 ripe avocado
5 ounces smoked salmon

1. Put the flour, eggs, spinach leaves, milk, and wasabi in a food processor and blend for 1–2 minutes to make the batter. It should be slightly green from the spinach, and the color may intensify over time. If you don't have a food processor, leave the spinach out and add it to the dish later, and blend the mixture using a hand whisk.

2. Heat 1 teaspoon of oil in a medium-size nonstick pan and put a quarter of the batter in, shaking the pan so the batter evens out; it should be around ⅛-inch thick. We like olive or coconut oil, but use whatever you prefer.

3. Cook for 2–4 minutes on each side. It should be obvious when the crepe is ready to be flipped as it will start to come away from the pan. Repeat the process to make 3 more.

4. Mash or slice the avocado and place some on each crepe along with a slice or two of smoked salmon. If you left the spinach out of the batter, put this on top, then fold the crepe in half.

32

SWEET ROASTED CHINESE CASHEWS

[feeling fragile choice]

Quick and easy, this nutritious snack boosts my energy levels. The cashews are rich in magnesium and vitamin B_6. Some of the ingredients might be new to you . . . they certainly were to me. They are available in most supermarkets now, though, and it is definitely worth tracking them down. Chinese five-spice powder consists of star anise, cinnamon, fennel, black pepper, and clove, while tamari sauce is made from fermented soybeans, like soy sauce, but it doesn't contain wheat. They both have fascinating histories and rich flavors.

A word of warning: the nuts can be quite sticky, but that makes them fun to eat.

– Makes around 6 portions –

5 ounces cashews
1 teaspoon Chinese five-spice powder
2 teaspoons tamari or soy sauce
2 teaspoons maple syrup or honey

1. Preheat the oven to 325°F.

2. Mix all the ingredients together in a bowl, then spread the nuts evenly over a baking sheet. You may want to line it with parchment paper to prevent them from sticking.

3. Roast them for 15 minutes, turning them halfway through. They should turn a dark brown as they caramelize, so give them a little longer if you think they need it. They'll be soft and sticky when you take them out, but leave them for 30 minutes and they'll soon harden up.

WALNUT AND ARUGULA PESTO WITH EDAMAME

For years, these young soybeans (pronounced ay-duh-MAH-me) were only to be found in Japanese restaurants, but they're now far more widely available. You can buy them already shelled, but I enjoy the peaceful process of shucking them. Now that I have embraced eating more mindfully, I like focusing on the elements of our recipes that particularly lend themselves to being done in a conscious way. A rich source of protein, choline, complex carbohydrates, and fiber, edamame releases energy slowly and the beans are a pretty shade of grassy green. If you struggle to find them, you can use fava beans instead. Any leftover pesto is handy to spread over fish and chicken to brighten up a simple meal.

– Serves 2, with leftover pesto –

5 ounces frozen edamame
3½ ounces arugula
2 ounces walnuts
Juice of ¼ lemon
5 Tablespoons olive oil
1 garlic clove
1 Tablespoon grated Parmesan, cheddar,
  or goat cheese (optional)

1. Either boil or steam the edamame for 5 minutes or until the beans are soft.

2. While they are cooking, combine the rest of the ingredients in a food processor or blender, and blend until smooth. If you don't have either, this process can be done in a mortar and pestle, which will produce a slightly thicker but no less delicious result. Add the cheese if you want a creamier version, though we don't think it is necessary.

3. Serve the pesto alongside the cooked beans— 1 rounded tablespoon of pesto is about the right amount for a serving of edamame.

CREAMY SWEET POTATO AND RED PEPPER SOUP

This colorful and flavorsome soup is rich in vitamin C and easy to make. It is a dish to combine with our *Iron-Rich Steak Salad*, to help the body to absorb the iron. The ingredients also supply vitamin A, magnesium, B vitamins, and antioxidants. Have it either as a cozy supper with friends or, if you halve the ingredients, as lunch for two. Harissa is a North African hot chili pepper paste, an exotic medley of various herbs and spices, and is an easy way to add kick to a familiar base.

– Serves 4 –

4 large red peppers (preferably slender Romano,
  but bell is fine), halved and seeded
2 Tablespoons olive oil
2 red onions, finely diced
2 teaspoons harissa paste
1½ pounds sweet potatoes, peeled and diced
1 quart vegetable or chicken stock
4 Tablespoons crème fraîche

1. Preheat the oven to 350°F and place the red peppers in a roasting dish with a splash of olive oil. Bake them for 20 minutes, or until they start to brown, turning them halfway through.

2. Heat a tablepoon of the oil in a medium pan and cook the onion and harissa on high heat. Stir occasionally to ensure that the onions do not burn.

3. Once the onions have started to caramelize, add the sweet potatoes and a little more oil and cook for 10 minutes.

4. Add the stock and bring it to a boil, then reduce the heat to a simmer. Remove the peppers from the oven and add them to the pan. Simmer gently until the sweet potatoes are cooked through.

5. Remove the soup from the heat and whiz it in a blender.

6. Serve it with a dollop of crème fraîche and a drizzle of olive oil.

PROSCIUTTO-WRAPPED SALMON WITH ROASTED RED CABBAGE AND SWEET POTATOES

I often choose this vibrantly colored dish when I am cooking for others and want it to feel like a special occasion. The sweet potatoes are a good slow-release carbohydrate and coupled with the protein provide steady energy.

– Serves 2 –

For the sweet potato fries:
1 pound sweet potatoes (2 large potatoes),
   cut into strips
2 Tablespoons olive oil
1 sprig of rosemary, leaves only

For the roasted red cabbage:
1 pound red cabbage, cut into ¼-inch–thick
   slices
3 Tablespoons olive oil
1 Tablespoon maple syrup or honey

2 salmon fillets
6 slices of prosciutto or Parma ham

1. Preheat the oven to 350°F. Ideally, it is better to use a convection oven for this to ensure the moisture is removed as the vegetables cook.

2. Place the sweet potato fries on a baking sheet and toss them with the olive oil and the rosemary. Then spread them in a single layer so they don't touch each other—this will make them crispier.

3. Bake for 25–35 minutes, turning them halfway through. If they seem soggy, don't panic—the edges should crisp up toward the end.

4. While the sweet potato is cooking, put the red cabbage on a large baking sheet and toss it with the olive oil and maple syrup, ensuring the leaves get an even coating and that they aren't too bunched together. Add these to the oven. The cooking time for the cabbage will vary depending on how hot and dry your oven is—normally 25–35 minutes.

5. After around 15 minutes, toss the cabbage with a spatula and let any excess moisture out of the oven as you do so. You'll see the cabbage diminish in size and start to crunch up as it caramelizes.

6. Meanwhile, remove the skin from the salmon using a sharp knife. There are plenty of videos online showing how to do this, or you could ask your fishmonger to do it for you. Of course, if you don't mind salmon skin, leave it on under the prosciutto.

7. Firmly wrap each salmon fillet with 3 pieces of prosciutto and place them on some foil or parchment paper.

8. Bake the fish in the hot oven for 10–12 minutes—you may need to remove either the sweet potatoes or the cabbage (or both, if they are cooked) from the oven. The ham may look dry from the outside, but inside the fish will be succulent.

9. Remove the salmon from the oven and leave it to rest while you put the baking sheets with the red cabbage and sweet potatoes back into the oven for 3–5 minutes to heat through, then serve.

SATISFYING SHRIMP PENNE WITH BROCCOLI

If you use whole wheat or spelt pasta, you are unlikely to suffer the same dip in energy that can be caused by eating refined carbohydrates such as white pasta. Apparently, pasta releases glucose more slowly into the system if you cook it al dente. I find it tastes better too. In this recipe, the protein in the shrimp helps to slow down the release of sugar. Shrimp also contain a compound called astaxanthin. This red pigment is found in certain marine plants and animals, and scientists have studied how it might benefit health, particularly in the treatment of immune, cardiovascular, and inflammatory diseases. There's more about this in our *Mental Clarity* chapter. If you are not keen on spicy foods, omit the chili flakes, and if you find the sauce a little too bitter, reduce the amount of lemon juice. Try to reheat the pasta the following day if there's any left over since, having been cooled after cooking, it contains more resistant starch, which can improve our gut health. I explain more about resistant starch in our *Nice and Calm* chapter.

– Serves 2 –

11–12 ounces spelt or whole wheat penne
1 Tablespoon olive oil
½ onion, finely sliced
2 garlic cloves, finely sliced
½ teaspoon chili flakes (optional)
1 small head of broccoli (or 10 broccolini
  spears), chopped into ¾-inch chunks
5 ounces asparagus tips, chopped into
  ¾-inch chunks
Juice of ½ lemon
⅓ cup white wine (the alcohol evaporates
  so it is fine for your mood)
⅓ cup fish stock or vegetable stock,
  if easier
1 ounce fresh parsley, chopped
5 ounces raw shrimp
Chili oil (a vegetable oil that has been
  infused with chili peppers—optional)

1. Cook the pasta according to the package instructions. Whole wheat takes a little longer than white.

2. Fry the onion, garlic, and chili flakes for 2 minutes in the olive oil, before adding the broccoli and asparagus. Cook for a further 5 minutes, or until the vegetables have softened but are still al dente.

3. Squeeze in the lemon juice and add the white wine, fish stock, and parsley.

4. Turn the heat down, add the shrimp, and simmer for 5 minutes more.

5. Stir the shrimp and vegetables through the cooked pasta. If you prefer a spicier dish, drizzle with chili oil before serving, or add some more dried chili flakes.

IRON-RICH STEAK SALAD

Alice used to find it quite hard to cook steak, but this method (inspired by Nigella Lawson) keeps it deliciously tender. The combination of the iron-rich steaks, the colorful salad, the zingy horseradish, and the creamy feta cheese is perfect. I use artichokes and sun-dried tomatoes from my local supermarket's deli counter, which saves a lot of time. Be sure not to buy artichokes soaked in vinegar, though, as the flavor will overpower the salad. If possible, use grass-fed steak, which contains more nutrients than intensively farmed beef.

– Serves 2 –

For the dressing:
1 Tablespoon Worcestershire sauce
1 Tablespoon crème fraîche
1 teaspoon prepared horseradish
1 teaspoon cider vinegar
1 teaspoon honey
1 teaspoon olive oil

2 x 9- to 10-ounce rump steaks, ideally
   around 1½ inches thick

For the marinade:
½ ounce fresh flat-leaf parsley, chopped
2 garlic cloves, crushed
6 Tablespoons extra-virgin olive oil
Juice and grated zest of ½ lemon
4 drops Tabasco sauce (optional)

For the salad:
3 ounces fresh flat-leaf parsley, chopped
6 sun-dried tomatoes, roughly chopped
4 artichoke hearts, quartered
4 ounces arugula
8 radishes, thinly sliced
3 ounces feta cheese, crumbled
4 Tablespoons pomegranate seeds (optional)
2 Tablespoons toasted pine nuts (optional)

1. First make the dressing by combining all the ingredients and shaking them together in a jar.

2. Trim the harder fat off the steaks, brush them with oil, and season both sides with a little salt.

3. Heat a griddle or heavy-based pan, and when hot add the meat. Cook for 4 minutes on each side. If you prefer your steak well-done, then leave it for another 1–2 minutes on each side.

4. Meanwhile, make the marinade. Whisk together all the ingredients in a dish big enough to accommodate the cooked steaks.

5. Place the steaks in the marinade for 8 minutes, turning them halfway through. Then remove them to a cutting board and slice them thinly on the diagonal.

6. While the meat rests, combine the salad ingredients except the pine nuts in a large bowl. Pour over three-quarters of the dressing and toss everything together.

7. To serve, place the sliced steak on a bed of the salad and pour over the rest of the dressing. Scatter with toasted pine nuts, if so desired.

BALANCED ENERGY: ESSENTIAL FOODS

Substitutes for refined sugar	Coconut sugar, brown rice syrup, maple syrup, date syrup, and honey. You will find more substitutions in our **Comfort Food** chapter. It is important to emphasize that "natural" sugars are still sugar. Even these should be eaten in moderate amounts.
Lower-sugar fruits	Berries, kiwis, pears, apples, oranges, lemons, and limes.
Chromium-rich foods	Barley, oats, green beans, sesame seeds, broccoli, bran cereal, wheat germ, egg yolk, tomatoes, and grape juice.
Slow-release carbohydrates	Brown rice, quinoa, sweet potatoes, rye flakes, low-sugar muesli or granola, oatmeal, rye bread, oatcakes, spelt or whole wheat pasta, and whole wheat flour. You will find more substitutions in our **Comfort Food** chapter.
Fiber-rich foods	Sweet potatoes, oats, flaxseeds, spinach, broccoli, figs, plums, and artichokes.
Proteins for snacks	Almonds, cashews, walnuts, pumpkin seeds, sunflower seeds, hummus, edamame, cottage cheese, miso, ham, chicken, and cooked shrimp.
Iron-rich foods	Red meat (lean beef, lamb, pork, venison), chicken livers, chickpeas, hummus, edamame, black beans, prunes, dried apricots, black quinoa, dates, kale, watercress, spinach, and dark chocolate.
Vitamin C	Oranges, grapefruits, lemons, broccoli, papayas, kiwis, asparagus, peppers, parsley, kale, apples, and pears.

BALANCED ENERGY: MEAL PLANNER

Breakfast	Nutritiously Nutty Granola Tropical Vitamin C Smoothie Two boiled eggs with half an avocado and a slice of pumpernickel or rye bread, with a thin spread of butter.
Morning snack	Almond and Toasted Pecan Spread on oatcakes, or with natural yogurt.
Lunch	Spelt and Spinach Crepes with Avocado Creamy Sweet Potato and Red Pepper Soup Satisfying Shrimp Penne with Broccoli Steamed or roasted fillet of fish served with broccoli and red peppers on a bed of arugula and quinoa, drizzled with olive oil, apple cider vinegar, and lemon juice.
Afternoon snack	Sweet Roasted Chinese Cashews Walnut and Arugula Pesto with Edamame
Dinner	Iron-Rich Steak Salad Prosciutto-Wrapped Salmon with Roasted Red Cabbage and Sweet Potatoes
Desserts	Almond and Toasted Pecan Spread with some fruit or yogurt Take a look at our **Comfort Food** chapter for other desserts that will keep your blood sugar balanced.
Drinks	Ginseng or jasmine tea

From "The Darkling Thrush"

At once a voice arose among
    The bleak twigs overhead
In a full-hearted evensong
    Of joy illimited;
An aged thrush, frail, gaunt, and small,
    In blast-beruffled plume,
Had chosen thus to fling his soul
    Upon the growing gloom.

Thomas Hardy

beating the blues

My mood, like anyone's, still dips occasionally, particularly early in the morning, when I can feel scared of getting out from under my duvet, and then late in the afternoon. The color seems to drain temporarily from my surroundings much like in "The Darkling Thrush." Despite the thrush being "aged," "frail, gaunt, and small," it is still capable of singing with "joy illimited," and I aspire to be able to do the same.

Medicinal herbs

Alice and I discussed using medicinal herbs such as Saint-John's-wort (named after St. John's Day, June 24, about when the plant starts to flower) and rhodiola to beat these low moods. Both are thought to boost our spirits, and therefore can be prescribed in pill form for depression. Research from London's Royal College of Psychiatrists suggests that one of the ingredients in Saint-John's-wort, hyperforin, can boost the brain's serotonin levels, hence causing this antidepressant effect.

After a lot of discussions with Alice and others, however, I decided to avoid both. I was keen to explore the power of food, not pills, as I thought that this would be a more long-term and more enjoyable solution.

Stimulating my appetite

The first step in tackling the times when I felt low was to improve my appetite. Alice suggested I start my bleaker mornings with hot water, lemon, and ginger, included here as our *Zesty Morning Kick-Start*. When I feel brave enough, I even add a dash of cayenne pepper to the mix. I found the drink helped to get my appetite going. Our digestive fluids may be affected when we are feeling glum, or worrying about the day ahead. Other people may find they get heartburn when they feel low, possibly due to acid in the stomach getting into places like the esophagus where it shouldn't be.

Another tip was to stir a tablespoon of good-quality apple cider vinegar into a small glass of water, to drink before a big meal. Bitter and peppery foods like arugula, grapefruit, basil, and mustard all helped my appetite improve and were extras to include at mealtimes on days I didn't feel hungry. Our *Zingy Zucchini, Pea, and Coconut Soup* not only makes me buoyant because it is such a bright acid green, it is also one of my favorite appetite-boosting dishes.

I learned to eat easily digestible foods throughout the day, such as Alice's *Happy Smoothie*. Herbal teas ease my digestion too. Dandelion root tea may improve bile production, which is essential in the digestion of fats. I am pleased that there's now a use for weeds from the garden.

Eating enough protein

Another way to tackle feeling low was to make sure I was eating enough protein. The building blocks of protein, the amino acids, are important for our brain, helping to make our neurotransmitters. We need to get this from a variety of sources, as we have seen in the Golden Rules. Try our recipes for *Salmon and Flaxseed Pancakes* (the flaxseed also contains omega-3s) or *Spiced Tomato Poached Eggs with Sweet Potato and Guacamole* to keep your protein stores up.

Supporting my serotonin levels

Serotonin is the so-called happiness hormone—a neurotransmitter or chemical messenger that plays an important role in both our brain and our digestive system. Indeed, although some serotonin is made in the brain, around 90 percent of it is found in the gut. Quite the multitasker, it also contributes to the functioning of our cardiovascular system, the formation of our bones, and the contraction of our muscles, all of which can indirectly boost our mental health by improving our physical health.

Serotonin and the gut

The serotonin in the gut helps with a number of important digestive functions, in particular the gut's natural movements that break up and digest food and ensure we have regular daily movements (sorry). Research suggests that serotonin levels may be linked to some gastrointestinal symptoms, including constipation, diarrhea, and conditions such as irritable bowel syndrome. Given the potential links between the health of our digestive system and the mind, it makes sense to ensure our gut has the right balance of serotonin.

How can what we eat affect our serotonin levels? A few foods actually contain serotonin, albeit in low amounts. These include walnuts, bananas, kiwis, plums, and tomatoes. Far more numerous, however, are the foods that can increase levels of tryptophan,

the amino acid from which serotonin is made and which itself is important to brain function. There is some evidence to suggest that low levels of tryptophan may play a role in depression. Studies have shown that if you feed animals meals containing all the essential amino acids except tryptophan, their serotonin becomes depleted.

Tryptophan is found predominantly in protein-rich foods like turkey, tuna, and natural yogurt, and also in oats, potatoes, sesame seeds, butternut squash seeds, sunflower seeds, and pumpkin seeds.

If that seems like a lot to remember, whiz up one of our aptly named *Happy Smoothies*: its yogurt and pumpkin seeds provide tryptophan and its bananas serotonin, while the yogurt should also help nourish your healthy bacteria—a good plan, since healthy gut flora seem to promote serotonin synthesis. You can read more about this in our **Nice and Calm** chapter.

Serotonin and the brain

The serotonin in our brain helps to relay messages from one area of it to another. Serotonin directly or indirectly influences our millions and millions of brain cells. Not sure exactly how many—it's disputed—but we have many more than 40 million! These include the ones related to happiness, sexual desire, and sleep, or, as one neuroscientist put it, all the things that are worth living for!

Some studies show that people who suffer recurrent and serious depression have depleted serotonin levels. This is why they are prescribed antidepressant drugs known as selective serotonin reuptake inhibitors (SSRIs), which are thought to work by increasing serotonin supplies in the brain.

Today, however, scientists are less certain about exactly how these antidepressants work, and few believe their effectiveness is wholly linked to their serotonin-boosting properties. Other neurotransmitters such as norepinephrine (also called noradrenaline) may also be involved.

Setting aside how antidepressants may or may not work, we need to address the question of how else to support our brain's supply of serotonin through diet.

I'm afraid this is tricky, and scientists still aren't really sure of the exact answer. Every drop of blood is filtered before it is allowed to flow through the blood–brain barrier—the security system the brain has for keeping out foreign substances. Serotonin that has been created in the digestive system isn't able to travel across the blood–brain barrier.

However, while pure serotonin is turned away at our brain's gate, tryptophan is not. You might now think, "Ah! So if I eat more tryptophan, I will boost my brain's supply of serotonin." Unfortunately, the answer is once again more complicated. It turns out that the other amino acids from the protein-rich foods mentioned above compete with the tryptophan to enter the brain. Our poor, old brain can't cope with all the competing amino acids knocking on the door, and don't let the tryptophan in.

So what can we do? There is some limited evidence that eating carbohydrates may help facilitate the transport of tryptophan into the brain. But we need much more research before we can simply say a carbohydrate-rich diet alleviates depression. Apart from anything else, eating too much refined carbohydrate can lead to type 2 diabetes, which itself can cause depression!

Snacking on foods that have a high proportion of tryptophan compared to other amino acids may be the answer, especially seeds such as sesame and pumpkin. One small study found that those who ate butternut squash seeds experienced reduced social anxiety disorder.

Scientists also think there may be a link between reduced serotonin levels and low intakes of vitamin D and omega-3 fatty acids. This in turn might lead to an increased risk of neuropsychiatric disorders and depression. Read on for more about the ways vitamin D and omega-3s help beat the blues, and try our *Vitamin D Mushroom and Mustard Soup* or our *Omega-3 Kedgeree*.

Given how hard it is to use diet to affect the serotonin in the brain, we need to find other ways to do it. Research has shown that both sunshine and exercise may boost serotonin production and its release. For me, and for millions of other people, a brisk walk in the sun is one of the best ways to beat the blues.

Vitamin B and vitamin D

Meanwhile, having a steady supply of B vitamins has helped my low moods, I suspect because of their role in supporting the nervous system. Our *Vitamin B Marmite-Roasted Pumpkin Seeds* and *Creamy Chicken and Brown Rice Soup* are good sources of B vitamins. Another vitamin that's helped boost my mood is vitamin D. Many depressed people have low vitamin D levels. Studies have not been able to show that taking vitamin D helps beat depression specifically. However, it helps so many other bodily processes that I, like the Department of Health, recommend making sure you get enough. Levels of vitamin D deficiency in Britain are the highest in 50 years, with one in five of us suffering severe deficiency. It is linked to an increased risk of heart disease, bowel cancer, breast cancer, multiple sclerosis, and diabetes.

Once I increased the amount of vitamin D I consumed, I felt better. I noticed I fell ill with colds and flu less often. My nails didn't crack and my skin glowed. Unsurprisingly, after years of looking rather gray, a peachier complexion helped my morale.

Government guidelines in the UK now recommend that from October to March we take a vitamin D supplement. During the summer months the majority of us should be able to get most of our vitamin D from sunlight, but the Department of Health recommends that those at high risk, including pregnant women, people who cover up their skin, and those who don't go outdoors, take supplements all year round.

Supplements have come in for quite a lot of criticism in recent years. In 2013, experts analyzed some of the world's most comprehensive research about multivitamin supplements, which involved half a million people. The conclusion? They were almost always a waste of money. That said, I know many who find supplements helpful if they lead rushed lives and struggle to eat well.

My view is that it is always better to get our vitamins from food if possible, though I have used supplements in the past. And the fact is that for many people a lack of exposure to the sun means that it is difficult to get healthy levels of vitamin D through diet alone. Unless you eat 10mg of it a day, equivalent to two and a half cans of tuna, one salmon fillet, or ten eggs, you should take a supplement. So I make an exception when it comes to vitamin D and happily pop a pill. I take a belt-and-suspenders approach and also try to eat foods that are rich in it. Welcome to our *Vitamin D Mushroom and Mustard Soup*. I like taking some to work in a thermos if I am going to be at my desk all day.

Zinc

Our family has always believed in the importance of zinc. A great-uncle and -aunt, both doctors, lived into their late nineties and always attributed their longevity to their zinc consumption. Zinc helps us with many functions, including making new cells and enzymes, and plays a role in the central nervous system. It is also thought to help brain cells communicate through neural pathways, a process known as "neuronal plasticity," and heighten concentration, as we will see in our **Mental Clarity** chapter. Zinc imbalances have been identified as contributors to a wide range of brain diseases, from Alzheimer's to depression. The element is found in high concentrations in the hippocampus. The etymology of *hippocampus*, incidentally, is endearing: the Greek *hippos* (horse) and *kampos* (sea monster) allude to its resemblance to a sea horse. The hippocampus regulates emotions, maintains the brain's protective barrier, and modulates aspects of our stress response system. So I wasn't surprised when I learned that zinc deficiency could be linked to depression and reduced focus—see our **Nutrition Note** below. Oysters, salmon, scallops, spinach, cashew nuts, and pumpkin and sesame seeds are all (among many others) useful sources of zinc; our *Salmon and Shrimp Teriyaki Skewers with Soba Noodles and Zucchini Ribbons* recipe contains a fair few of these.

Healthy fats and omega-3

Healthy fats, as discussed in our Golden Rules, may be important in improving mood. Omega-3, in particular, is crucial, which is why this chapter contains four oily fish recipes: *Omega-3 Kedgeree, Salmon and Flaxseed Pancakes, Salmon and Shrimp Teriyaki Skewers with Soba Noodles and Zucchini Ribbons*, and *Smoked Mackerel and Horseradish Pâté with Oatcakes*.

On some mornings, if it is mild, I eat a bowl of kedgeree outside in our back garden and remind myself of Hardy's poem. The healing power of nature, like poetry, is another companion to the restorative nature of nourishment. Sometimes I even spot a joyful thrush.

Summing up—to help my low mood, I:

stimulated my appetite

ate enough protein to help the chemical messengers in my brain

supported my serotonin levels

upped my consumption of B vitamins and vitamin D

consumed more zinc

consumed more healthy fats

Nutrition Note: zinc and depression

In a randomized trial in 2013, participants were given either 25mg of zinc or a placebo alongside antidepressants, for 12 weeks. Those in the zinc group had significantly reduced scores in the Beck Depression Inventory (a questionnaire used to assess a patient's mood, in which higher scores indicate higher levels of depression) compared to the placebo group.

ZESTY MORNING KICK-START

Though not always tempting for me, I have found that this drink boosts my appetite. The ginger and cayenne contain helpful anti-inflammatory compounds.

– Serves 1 –

¼–½ lemon, to taste
Pinch of ground cayenne pepper (get good-quality organic stuff if you can)
¼ inch gingerroot, chopped or grated (we find it easiest to use a peeler to get fine flakes)

Squeeze the juice from the lemon wedge into a mug, add the pepper and ginger, and top up with hot water. Let it stand for 1–2 minutes, then enjoy as soon as it has cooled down a little.

Feeling strong? Add 1 teaspoon of apple cider vinegar. *Feeling sensitive?* Add 1 teaspoon of honey, preferably manuka.

HAPPY SMOOTHIE

Handy for a light breakfast or afternoon snack, with raw cacao powder as a tasty ingredient. Cocoa powder is a decent substitute, but isn't thought to have as many health-giving properties. Cacao contains magnesium and other antioxidants, and there has been much interest recently in its potential benefits, including its effect on blood pressure. The yogurt and pumpkin seeds provide tryptophan and the banana serotonin, which explains this smoothie's name.

– Serves 1 –

½ medium banana
½ cup raspberries (frozen are fine)
1 ounce spinach leaves
2 Tablespoons natural yogurt
½ teaspoon ground cinnamon
1 heaping Tablespoon raw cacao powder, or
  good-quality unsweetened cocoa powder
1 heaping Tablespoon pumpkin seeds
Milk, or dairy-free alternative, to top up
1 heaping Tablespoon maple syrup or honey
  to sweeten (optional)

Combine all the ingredients in a blender and blitz until smooth.

CREAMY CHICKEN AND BROWN RICE SOUP

Nourishing and comforting on cold days, this soup has become a family favorite. Brown rice delivers B vitamins, while chicken is a source of protein, which helps make neurotransmitters for the brain, as well as selenium, which can cheer us up and help our mental functioning. What's more, the Chinese have been using celery to treat anxiety for thousands of years.

– Serves 2–3 –

1 Tablespoon salted butter
2 celery sticks, thinly sliced
2 carrots, thinly sliced
1 small onion, finely chopped
2 garlic cloves, finely chopped
3 sprigs of thyme
1 Tablespoon whole wheat flour
3 handfuls of brown rice
2 cups chicken stock—you can add a
  bit more if there doesn't seem to be
  enough liquid
2 chicken breasts, already cooked
  (roasted, sautéed, or poached is
  easiest) and shredded
1 ounce fresh flat-leaf parsley, chopped
2 Tablespoons heavy cream

1. Melt the butter in a large pan and add the celery, carrots, onion, garlic, and thyme. Cook over moderate heat for 8 minutes, stirring often. Add a little water to the pan if you need more moisture.

2. Sprinkle the flour over the vegetables and continue to cook for around 2 minutes. Stir occasionally to prevent burning. You may need to add a tablespoon of the stock if it seems to be sticking too much.

3. Rinse the rice thoroughly in a sieve under the tap and then add it to the pan. Gradually stir in the stock, adding a little water if the mixture seems too thick. Bring to a boil, then gently simmer over low heat for 20 minutes, stirring occasionally.

4. Add the cooked chicken and parsley, then simmer for another 10 minutes, or until the rice is cooked.

5. Take the pan off the heat and stir in the cream.

6. Discard the thyme sprigs and ladle the soup into bowls.

SPICED TOMATO POACHED EGGS WITH SWEET POTATO AND GUACAMOLE

This protein-rich recipe makes for a cheerful weekend brunch on a cold morning. Or serve it with whole wheat tortillas and sour cream for a more substantial lunch or dinner. The guacamole is optional, depending upon how much time you have, and your personal preference.

– Serves 2 –

For the eggs:
1 Tablespoon olive oil
1 red onion, finely chopped
2 garlic cloves, finely sliced
½ red chili, seeded and chopped (use more or less, depending on your preference)
1 teaspoon tomato paste
1 ounce fresh flat-leaf parsley, chopped
Dash of red wine
½ teaspoon paprika (optional)
1 red bell pepper, seeded and finely chopped
½ medium-size sweet potato, chopped into ¾-inch chunks
1½ 14-ounce cans chopped tomatoes
4 eggs

For the guacamole:
1 ripe avocado (or more, if you want extra portions)
Juice of ½ lime
¼ red chili, seeded and chopped
1 ounce fresh cilantro, chopped
Dash of olive oil
1 Tablespoon grated Parmesan, to serve

1. Heat the olive oil in a shallow pan with a lid and gently soften the onion, garlic, and chili. Add a little water if necessary to prevent them from burning.

2. After 2 minutes, stir in the tomato paste, parsley, red wine, paprika, pepper, and sweet potato. Simmer for 2 minutes (add a splash more water if necessary) before adding the chopped tomatoes.

3. Cook for around 15 minutes, by which point the potatoes and peppers should be softening nicely. The mixture should be the consistency of a thick stew.

4. Create a little dip in the mixture and crack an egg into it, then do the same with the other 3 eggs. Try to get the eggs evenly spaced out and not too close to the base of the pan, to prevent them from burning.

5. Put the lid on and let the eggs poach in the stew on low heat for a further 3–4 minutes. You may want to spoon some of the stew over the eggs to ensure the tops cook properly, but take care not to overcook them.

6. Meanwhile, make the guacamole by mashing the avocado in a bowl and then mixing in the rest of the ingredients except for the cheese.

7. Divide the egg mixture between two bowls, and serve it with a sprinkle of Parmesan and the guacamole on the side.

VITAMIN D MUSHROOM AND MUSTARD SOUP

Mushrooms make vitamin D in response to sunlight, so leave them out to sunbathe for as long as you like before you make the soup. We use a variety of mushrooms in this recipe, all of which have different tastes and textures.

Shiitake mushrooms come from Asia and are traditionally grown on hardwood logs such as oak. Oyster mushrooms look rather like silvery-gray ears, and like shiitake have a meaty texture. Both shiitake and oyster have medicinal properties. Porcini mushrooms have a strong nutty flavor and are much used in Italian cooking. They can be rather expensive, so, if you prefer, substitute white button mushrooms, which are just as nutritious and may have extra benefits for your mood, as you can read in our *Nutrition Note* at the end of the recipe.

Leave the skin on the parsnips for extra fiber and goodness. Feel free to use rutabagas or turnips as an alternative to parsnips, and substitute cream or Greek yogurt for the mascarpone.

– Serves 4 –

10 dried porcini mushrooms
1¼ pounds mixed mushrooms (oyster, shiitake, button), roughly chopped
2 Tablespoons olive oil
1 red onion, sliced
2 garlic cloves, chopped
3 parsnips, chopped
¼ cup white wine
3 cups vegetable or chicken stock
3 ounces fresh parsley
1 Tablespoon prepared mustard
1½ Tablespoons mascarpone cheese

1. Pour ¾ cup boiling water over the porcini mushrooms in a bowl, cover, and let them soak for 20 minutes.

2. Wash the fresh mushrooms and, if you have time, leave them to dry in uninterrupted (no windows or glass) sunlight for as long as you are able to. This increases their vitamin D content.

3. Heat the olive oil in a large saucepan and add the red onion. Cook it on medium heat for 3–4 minutes, then stir in the garlic and parsnips.

4. When the onions have softened, add the fresh mushrooms and cook for another minute, then pour in the white wine.

5. Drain the liquid from the porcini mushrooms into another bowl, then add them to the pan. Sieve the liquid a few times to remove any grit before pouring it into the pan along with the stock.

6. Turn down the heat, cover the pan with a lid, and let it simmer for 20–30 minutes, or until all the ingredients are soft.

7. Remove the pan from the heat and add the parsley and mustard, then blend the soup to your preferred consistency using an immersion blender. Don't blend it for too long, or you will lose the texture of the mushrooms.

8. Stir in the mascarpone (I sometimes add a little extra mustard too) before serving, or dollop it on top with a sprinkle of parsley once you have ladled the soup into bowls.

Nutrition Note: magic mushrooms

A controversial new piece of research has indicated that the psychedelic compound in magic mushrooms could one day be used to treat patients with severe depression who do not respond to other therapies. A very small-scale study of the use of psilocybin in cases of treatment-resistant depression showed that it was safe and effective. Of 12 patients given the drug, all showed some decrease in symptoms of depression for at least three weeks, while 7 continued to show a positive response after three months—and 5 remained in remission beyond that time. Robin Carhart-Harris, who led the 2016 study at Imperial College London, said that the results published in *Lancet Psychiatry* were striking. Psilocybin acts on the serotonin system, suggesting that it could be developed for treating depression. There are no magic mushrooms in our vitamin D soup—yet.

The Chinese have been prescribing mushrooms for centuries. It is thought that mushrooms may contribute to the health of our digestive system. One study on mice found that eating button mushrooms had an effect on gut-microbial diversity. Good-quality trials are required to investigate whether they might have the same beneficial effect on humans.

SALMON AND SHRIMP TERIYAKI SKEWERS WITH SOBA NOODLES AND ZUCCHINI RIBBONS

A rather exotic recipe, which is rich in omega-3s and introduced me to several new flavors that I now like. Japanese teriyaki sauce—made from soy sauce, sake, sugar, and ginger—is probably the most basic of Asian marinades. If you can't get hold of teriyaki sauce, add three parts soy sauce (or tamari) to two parts maple syrup or honey. Soba noodles are made of buckwheat and have a low GI, but do use whole wheat if you can't find them. Japanese mirin, a type of rice wine, is high in sugar and used here to add sweetness to the dish.

– Serves 4 –

For the skewers:
5 Tablespoons teriyaki sauce
Juice and zest of 1 lime
2 Tablespoons sesame oil
1 garlic clove, finely chopped
1 teaspoon chopped gingerroot
1 Tablespoon Japanese mirin (optional, to add
  sweetness)
2 salmon fillets, skinned and sliced into
  2-inch chunks
5 ounces fresh jumbo shrimp (use smaller ones if
  you can't get jumbo, but ensure they are raw)
4 wooden or metal skewers (soak wooden ones
  in water before use to prevent charring)

For the noodles:
1 zucchini
7 ounces soba noodles
Juice of 1 lime
1 Tablespoon sesame oil
1 teaspoon teriyaki sauce
½ teaspoon dried chili flakes

To serve:
½ ounce fresh cilantro, chopped
1 green onion, finely sliced
1 Tablespoon roasted sesame seeds
  (optional)

1. In a large bowl, mix the teriyaki sauce, lime juice and zest, sesame oil, garlic, ginger, and mirin. Place the salmon and shrimp in the sauce. Marinate in the fridge for at least an hour.

2. Use a spiralizer to cut the zucchini into ribbons.

3. When you are ready to eat, heat the broiler or fire up the barbecue. Slide the fish and shrimp onto the skewers.

4. Put the noodles in a big pan of boiling water and cook for 3–5 minutes. When they are soft, drain them and run them under cold water (this stops them from sticking together). Set aside.

5. Grill the skewers several inches from the heat for 4–6 minutes, turning them halfway through and taking care not to overcook them.

6. Put the noodles back in the pan on low heat and stir in the zucchini ribbons and the rest of the noodle ingredients, and gently heat them through for 3–5 minutes.

7. Serve the skewers on the noodles, with a sprinkling of cilantro, green onion, and sesame seeds.

OMEGA-3 KEDGEREE

This traditional Indian dish of fish and rice became popular in England in the Victorian era, when British colonials returned home and started having it for breakfast. Our version works at all times of day, and is filled with omega-3 fats, zinc, and B vitamins. My mother said that this was one of the best kedgerees she'd ever had, and she's eaten a good number. This kedgeree can be reheated a day later and served for breakfast: those Victorians were on to something. It's useful on those dark days when I don't feel like eating or cooking first thing, but know it will help me feel more cheerful if I do. There's something comforting about serving this dish in an individual bowl, which you can cradle.

– Serves 3–4 –

4 eggs
½ cup low-fat milk
2 bay leaves
3 mackerel or salmon fillets
2 cups long-grain brown rice
2 Tablespoons olive oil
1 large onion, finely diced
2 garlic cloves, finely sliced
1 teaspoon ground coriander
1 teaspoon ground cumin
1 teaspoon ground turmeric (or fresh if you
  can get it, peeled and chopped)
2 heaped Tablespoons curry powder, or to taste
1 red chili, seeded and finely sliced
4 tomatoes, seeded and chopped
Juice of 1 lime
4 Tablespoons Greek yogurt
1 ounce fresh cilantro, chopped
1 ounce fresh parsley, chopped

1. Boil the eggs for 10 minutes, then run them under cold water to stop them cooking. Set them aside.

2. Put the milk, bay leaves, and fish fillets in a pan and add enough water to cover the fish. Bring to a boil, and then reduce to a simmer for roughly 5 minutes. Remove the pan from the heat and set aside.

3. Cook the rice according to the package instructions, drain it, rinse it in cold water, and then drain it again. Leave it in the fridge until it is needed.

4. Meanwhile, heat the olive oil in a large pan and add the onion, garlic, coriander, cumin, turmeric, curry powder, and chili. Let the mixture soften for about 10 minutes on low heat, adding a little water to the pan to keep the temperature low. Stir occasionally to make sure it doesn't burn. Then add the tomatoes and lime juice and simmer for 5 minutes.

5. Flake the fish into the pan; peel and quarter the eggs and add these and the rice too, and gently heat everything through.

6. Serve each portion with a dollop of Greek yogurt, a generous sprinkle of cilantro and parsley, and freshly ground black pepper (this may help you absorb the curcumin, the bright yellow chemical in the turmeric).

VITAMIN B MARMITE-ROASTED PUMPKIN SEEDS
[feeling fragile choice]

Even if you are not keen on Marmite, these are tempting. This is an easy recipe and one to turn to if you are feeling down and not up to much cooking. Marmite contains vitamin B_6, and the pumpkin seeds are a source of zinc, which are both important for the nervous system and supporting mood. I add the seeds to salads and snacks.

– Serves 5 –

2 teaspoons Marmite*, or a similar
  product, such as Vegemite
1 teaspoon honey or maple syrup (the
  latter is a bit thinner and easier to mix)
5 ounces pumpkin seeds

1. Preheat the oven to 325°F.

2. In a bowl, mix together the Marmite and maple syrup or honey and then stir in the pumpkin seeds, ensuring they get an even coating.

3. Lightly grease a baking sheet (or use parchment paper) and spread the pumpkin seed mixture evenly over it.

4. Bake the seeds for 8–10 minutes, stirring them halfway through. Keep a close watch on them, as they burn easily.

5. Remove them from the oven and spread them on a plate to dry for an hour before breaking them up and storing them in an airtight container. They may still be sticky—but that's the point.

*Available in international sections of some supermarkets, health-food or specialty stores, or online.

SALMON AND FLAXSEED PANCAKES

All of us like pancakes, surely? This recipe provides double helpings of omega-3, thanks to the salmon and the flaxseed. In the eighth century, King Charlemagne believed so strongly in the benefits of flaxseed that he passed a law requiring his subjects to consume it. While I wouldn't go that far, I would encourage you to hunt it down, as its nutty flavor boosts this recipe and will surely boost your mood.

– Serves 2 (around 4–5 pancakes) –

¾ cup spelt flour
1 heaped Tablespoon flaxseed meal
2 teaspoons baking powder
¾ cup plus 2 Tablespoons almond milk
1 egg
4 teaspoons coconut or olive oil
4 Tablespoons Greek yogurt
5 ounces smoked salmon

1. Combine the flour, flaxseed, baking powder, milk, and egg until you have a smooth batter.

2. Heat a frying pan and melt 1 teaspoon of coconut oil.

3. Pour 3 Tablespoons of the batter into the center of the pan and allow it to spread to around 6 inches in diameter—this should create the right degree of thickness, but if you want it thinner, tip the pan so it spreads farther.

4. Cook it for 2–3 minutes and then flip it over. The pancake will come away easily and you will see small pockets of air start to appear on the uncooked surface, which is a sign it will be nice and fluffy.

5. Remove the pancake once it is golden on both sides.

6. Repeat with the rest of the mixture.

7. Serve the pancakes immediately, topping each with 1 tablespoon of Greek yogurt and some of the smoked salmon.

SMOKED MACKEREL AND HORSERADISH PÂTÉ WITH OATCAKES

A non-recipe recipe, this pâté is so easy to make, and is a departure from the familiar, exceedingly fishy version from my youth. It has a nice kick to it, but you can cut out the chili if you are not keen on spice. If you can't get fresh mackerel, use canned—it is no less packed with omega-3s.

– Serves 5 –

1½ smoked mackerel fillets (I like the peppered ones)
1 teaspoon horseradish sauce
1 red chili, seeded and finely chopped
Juice and zest of 1 lemon
1 ounce fresh cilantro, chopped
2 Tablespoons Greek yogurt
10–12 oatcakes
1 green onion, finely chopped

1. Take the skin off the mackerel, trying not to lose all the healthy fatty bits that live between the skin and the flesh.

2. Break the mackerel into small pieces, removing any bones that are left in the flesh, and put it in a food processor.

3. Blitz the fish together with the horseradish, chili, lemon, cilantro, and yogurt. We like it smooth, but others prefer it with more texture. You can put it in the fridge for a while to thicken a little, or eat it as is.

4. Spread the pâté thickly on the oatcakes, and garnish with chopped green onion.

ZINGY ZUCCHINI, PEA, AND COCONUT SOUP

This soup is quick, fresh, and flavorsome and sure to tickle my taste buds, which are somewhat shy when I am low. There is plenty of protein in the peas, while the parsley, lime, and zucchini all boost the appetite. Coconut milk is a nice alternative to dairy, but you could use whole milk, cream, or crème fraîche if you prefer.

– Serves 3 –

8 large zucchini
1 green chili, seeded and roughly chopped
3 garlic cloves, roughly chopped
2 Tablespoons coconut oil
¾ cup plus 2 Tablespoons fresh or frozen peas
Juice and zest of 1 large lime
1 ounce fresh parsley, chopped
1½ cups canned coconut milk

1. Preheat the oven to 350°F.

2. Roughly chop the zucchini into 2-inch chunks.

3. Place them on a baking sheet with the chili and garlic.

4. Melt the coconut oil in a pan or in the oven, and then spread it evenly over the zucchini.

5. Bake for 20 minutes, or until the zucchini is soft but not overcooked, turning once halfway through.

6. Steam the peas until they are soft. This will take longer if they are fresh.

7. Put the lime juice and zest, parsley, and coconut milk (shake well before opening the can) into a large saucepan. I start by adding three-quarters of the coconut milk, and then add the rest if I want a smoother soup.

8. Add the cooked zucchini to the pan and use an immersion blender to blitz everything together. Then add the peas and blitz again. How smooth you want it is up to you, but we prefer it with a few lumps and bumps.

BEATING THE BLUES: ESSENTIAL FOODS

Possible digestive aids	Arugula, watercress, lemon, ginger, cayenne pepper, organic apple cider vinegar, dandelion tea, mint tea, and fennel tea.
Protein	Meat, fish, eggs, chickpeas, nuts, seeds, cottage cheese, tofu, tempeh, miso, beans, lentils, peas, brown rice, and hemp protein powder.
B vitamins	Eggs, beans, legumes, lentils, mushrooms, quinoa, oats, brown rice, and Marmite (or Vegemite).
Vitamin D	Mushrooms (try to leave them out in the sun before use), oily fish, red meat, egg yolks, and fortified cereals. In general, dietary sources contain only relatively small amounts.
Zinc	Sunflower seeds, pumpkin seeds, salmon, scallops, poultry, and squid.
Healthy fats	Herring, mackerel, fresh tuna, salmon, anchovies, sardines, trout, walnuts, flaxseed, hempseed, hempseed oil, chia seeds, broccoli, kale, and cauliflower.
Serotonin- and tryptophan-rich foods	Serotonin: walnuts, bananas, plums, kiwis, and tomatoes. Tryptophan: turkey, tuna, natural yogurt, oats, potatoes, sunflower seeds, and butternut squash seeds.

BEATING THE BLUES: MEAL PLANNER

Breakfast	Zesty Morning Kick-Start Happy Smoothie Spiced Tomato Poached Eggs with Sweet Potato and Guacamole Omega-3 Kedgeree One slice of pumpernickel bread with a thin spread of Marmite (or Vegemite) to taste.
Morning snack	Vitamin B Marmite-Roasted Pumpkin Seeds
Lunch	Salmon and Flaxseed Pancakes Salad of chicken, avocado, quinoa, and spinach leaves. For a dressing use olive oil, lemon, and apple cider vinegar. Vitamin D Mushroom and Mustard Soup with oatcakes and hummus or cottage cheese. Zingy Zucchini, Pea, and Coconut Soup with whole-grain toast.
Afternoon snack	Smoked Mackerel and Horseradish Pâté with Oatcakes Handful of seeds or nuts with dark chocolate.
Dinner	Mediterranean roasted vegetables (eggplant, zucchini, peppers, and red onion) with lentils, goat cheese, and toasted pumpkin seeds. Salmon and Shrimp Teriyaki Skewers with Soba Noodles and Zucchini Ribbons Creamy Chicken and Brown Rice Soup
Desserts	Almond and Toasted Pecan Spread with some fruit or yogurt. Take a look at our **Comfort Food** chapter for other desserts that will keep your blood sugar balanced.
Drinks	Water Dandelion or fennel or mint tea Fresh mint with hot water

From "A Boy's Song"

Where the pools are bright and deep,
Where the grey trout lies asleep,
Up the river and o'er the lea,
That's the way for Billy and me.

James Hogg

nice and calm

I often return to the poem "A Boy's Song" when I am feeling anxious. I find its evocation of boyhood and nature soothing, and enjoy the repetition of "That's the way for Billy and me." Although my mood is generally much steadier than it was, I can still sometimes feel actively panicked, as if for a moment I am metaphorically braced for a crash that never comes. It is different from feeling low.

Thank goodness I have found that nourishing a healthy gut by eating certain foods calms me down. Being overwhelmed was what triggered my depressive episodes, so I have been interested in the links between anxiety and our digestive system, which is such a promising area of research. This is rather a long chapter. Please bear with me—it might make a difference to your happiness too.

Supporting a healthy gut

The dangers of inflammation

There's some evidence from animal studies to suggest that when our guts are inflamed, it can affect our mood. Some of the small proteins that control this inflammation are known as cytokines. Though these are important molecules for many bodily processes, if too many of them escape from the gut into the rest of the body, they may cause inflammation elsewhere.

An elevated level of these cytokines has been linked with depression and is known as the cytokine hypothesis; read our **Nutrition Note** on page 72 for more information. The point to remember is that we want to prevent our digestive tracts from becoming inflamed.

Unhealthy bacteria

One way to reduce inflammation is to encourage healthy bacteria to flourish in the digestive system. It is thought that an increase in the levels of unhelpful or "bad" bacteria that emit chemicals can compromise the lining of the intestine, leading to a fairly self-explanatory condition known as increased intestinal permeability, or "leaky gut." This might allow some germs, toxins, and small undigested food particles into the blood, leading to inflammation, intolerances, and oxidative stress. However, this theory has not been conclusively proved and more research is necessary.

There may be a link between the bacteria in our digestive system and anxiety. The other **Nutrition Note** on page 72 explains how our gut bacteria can have an effect on our stress levels. In the future, it's possible that we will see the development of "psychobiotics," a catchy word for specific strains of bacteria that may support mental health. Some gastroenterologists already prescribe treatments traditionally given to those with low mood, such as antidepressants and cognitive behaviorial therapy, to patients with bowel disorders. It makes sense, given that our two "brains" are talking to one another.

So what do we need to eat to support a healthy gut? My approach has been twofold. First, cut down on the "bad" stuff, and second, increase the "good"— and please forgive these unscientific colloquialisms!

How to avoid the "bad" stuff

Sugar, alcohol, certain drugs such as antibiotics, fatty cuts of meat, burned foods, processed foods, and too much refined white carbohydrates are all thought to contribute to poor gut health.

Like many alarmed by talk of gluten sensitivity, I was worried I was eating too much bread and that it might be damaging my gut and making me anxious. Alice reassured me I need not give up on bread altogether. While she acknowledged the constant new research about sensitivity to gluten generally, she felt that for me, as for most people who don't suffer from the medically recognized celiac disease, a moderate intake of gluten from whole-grain sources about once a day would be fine. Furthermore, if I went completely gluten-free, I might risk vitamin deficiencies, in vitamin B in particular, and not be getting enough fiber, folic acid, iron, and zinc.

. . . and increase the "good" stuff

Start with anti-inflammatory omega-3s. We suggest in our **Meal Planner** in this chapter that you eat some grilled salmon or other oily fish, and you will find other recipes for oily fish in other chapters.

Nutrition Note: the gut, inflammation, and cytokines

Cytokines are small proteins that act as chemical messengers. They may enter the brain through the blood-brain barrier—the thin layer of cells separating the brain's blood from that of the body. It is thought that cytokines may then interfere with the chemical messaging or neurotransmission in our brain and the balance of serotonin and dopamine. The links between this response and depression and anxiety disorders has recently become a particular area of interest in scientific research, and a number of studies have found higher concentrations of these inflammatory cytokines circulating in patients with depression.

Having said that, not everyone who suffers from inflammation will in turn become depressed, and it is worth noting that not all types of depression involve cytokines. We respond as individuals depending on our genes, stress levels, hormones, and environment.

Nutrition Note: stress and gut bacteria

Studies have revealed close links between stress and the microbes living in our intestines. In a 2015 study from McMaster University in Canada, mice that were stressed by being separated from their mothers showed poor gut health, with their stomachs containing abnormal levels of stress hormones. While the research is on rodents, and often what applies to mice doesn't apply to humans, many scientists now think that stress has a strong effect on our gut bacteria and that these gut bacteria in turn can have a profound influence on our mental health.

Second, vary your supply of carbohydrates. I am now wary of white pasta, crackers, bread, and cereal—which had all been favorites of mine. I realized that these made up nearly two-thirds of my diet on some days. I now choose quinoa, brown rice, beans, legumes, oats, and starches from sweet potatoes or ordinary potatoes with their skins on for their fiber and nutrients.

Cooking foods like whole wheat pasta, rice, and potatoes and then allowing them to cool before reheating them changes the structure of the carbohydrate, leading to an increase in resistant starch, a form of fiber that provides a source of fuel for your good bacteria. Because this resistant starch travels through the digestive system nearly intact, it can also support regular bowel movements. These days I reheat leftovers of pasta, quinoa, or beans as much as possible.

Third, boost your supply of fruit and vegetables that contain fiber. An example in this chapter is our recipe for *Jeweled Guacamole and Roasted Peppers on Rye Bread*. A well-functioning gut needs different elements to digest food effectively, and the variety of vitamins and minerals in fruit and vegetables can help throughout the process. Later in this chapter I discuss the particularly helpful contribution of magnesium.

A final point on what we need for a healthy gut: we should ensure we eat enough pre- and probiotic foods, which help maintain the right balance of bacteria. Prebiotics are nondigestible foods that feed the growth of bacteria in the colon, found particularly in fermented vegetables and Jerusalem artichokes—see our **Nutrition Note** below. Probiotics are live bacteria and yeasts in yogurt, dairy products, and other foods, such as miso and kombucha, a type of fermented tea. They may also be taken in pills. Yogurt, ideally so thick it stands up in the bowl, is my own favorite probiotic. Read our other **Nutrition Note** below to find out more.

Nutrition Note: prebiotics
In a 2015 Oxford University study of healthy volunteers, one group was given one of two types of prebiotic, the other a placebo, and then both groups were tested after three weeks to see how they processed positive and negative information. Those who'd taken one type of the prebiotic (called Bimuno galactooligosaccharides, B-GOS) paid more attention overall to the positive information, and showed less anxiety when given the negative information. They had significantly less of the stress hormone cortisol in their saliva when they woke.

Nutrition Note: yogurt
A few years ago, a gastroenterologist called Emeran Mayer, based at the University of California, Los Angeles, worked with 36 healthy women for four weeks. Twelve of them ate a cup of a widely available fermented milk product otherwise known as yogurt, which contained four species of live probiotics, twice a day. Eleven ate a nonfermented milk product. The rest had neither. All the women were then shown several different facial expressions. Brain scans showed that those who ate the yogurt had calmer reactions to the images than both the groups that didn't. The results were published in 2013. The study authors suggest that gut microbes might affect our brain chemistry and our mood. It should be noted, however, that the authors received a grant from a yogurt company.

Other approaches that can help create a happy digestive system

What can we do beyond changing what we eat? I try to be less stressed generally, as I now realize the extent to which stress messes with my stomach as well as my head. When we are anxious, blood is pumped away from our gut, which has a negative effect on peristalsis (wavelike muscle contractions that move food along our digestive tracts). The muscles in our gut wall are sensitive, which is perhaps why a phrase such as "gut reaction" carries so much weight.

Exercise not only reduces our stress generally but may also help our guts. Though doctors warn we must be careful of extrapolating animal studies to humans, some animal studies suggest that exercise may have a beneficial effect on gut immune function and microbiome characteristics. Butyrate is a fatty substance produced by our gut microbes that benefits the immune system, and exercise stimulates microbes to produce more of it. Pleasingly, butter—especially from grass-fed cows—contains butyrate. So I enjoy a piece of whole-grain toast and butter now and then and sometimes cook with butter too.

There has also been some interest in how intermittent short-term fasting might help our microbes. Many animals fast naturally in the wild, and humans have been intermittently fasting for years in the name of religion. I haven't tried this approach since I need to eat steadily to stay energized, but if it is of interest to you, the research into it is well summarized in Dr. Michael Mosley's book *The Fast Diet*.

Finally, though it might not sound particularly appealing—don't read the next few lines if you are squeamish or about to do some cooking—recent research has shown that transplanting a microbiome through another person's fecal matter (containing healthier gut flora) could have positive results in those with damaged intestines. Since 2013, the US Food and Drug Administration has regulated feces as an experimental drug, and, though it is not something I have tried myself, it might eventually prove to work.

Once I started to change my diet and improve my gut health, I began to enjoy a virtuous circle whereby my mood influenced my digestion, which in turn affected my mood. The more relaxed I was, the more easily I digested and benefited from Good Mood Food.

I find that our *Uplifting Spiced Saffron Tea* can calm my gut as well as my nerves. As we saw in the Golden Rules, there's some evidence that saffron can help with anxiety. I like sipping the tea slowly from my favorite china cup: a peaceful pause in a busy day.

Reducing anxiety

Magnesium

As well as trying to nourish a healthy gut, I turn to particular minerals to ease my anxiety, chief among them magnesium. Magnesium is involved in a variety of processes in our body, including normal muscle function and maintaining our bones. It can contribute to the normal functioning of our nervous system and might help memory and cognition (we will come to this subject in our **Mental Clarity** chapter).

One 2006 study has suggested that a magnesium deficiency may contribute to irritability, nervousness, and depression. Magnesium might help to ease tension, and relieve muscular pain and headaches, which are common side effects of anxiety.

Leafy vegetables, sunflower seeds, whole-grain oats, quinoa, and brown rice all contain the super-helpful magnesium. We have included some of these ingredients in our *Nutty Spiced Quinoa Cooked Cereal* and *Calming Green Broth*, but let's face it, that's not as interesting as learning that magnesium can be found in raw cacao powder, and to a lesser extent in a piece of dark chocolate.

Of all the discoveries I have made about nutrition in the last few years, this one has made me especially happy. Cocoa products, including dark chocolate, might have some health benefit! Only the very good stuff, mind—in most chocolate, the potential benefit of some of these compounds is likely outweighed by the sugar and fat content. Still, I have found it a relief to know I can enjoy a square of dark chocolate containing 70 percent cocoa solids on occasion. On page 176 you will find a recipe for *Dark Chocolate Brazil Nut Brownies* and you will already have encountered our *Happy Smoothie* recipe, which contains raw cacao (page 52). Almonds are another source of magnesium, so choose dark chocolate with almonds if you can, and try our recipe for *Cinnamon, Almond, and Lamb Curry with Cilantro Brown Rice*.

Magnesium can be absorbed through the skin, and Epsom salts are rich in it. Taking an Epsom salts bath is a nourishing tonic and a soothing way to wind down at the end of the day.

Vitamin B$_6$

Vitamin B$_6$ is another stalwart that helps me when I am anxious. This may be because it plays a role in the synthesis of serotonin from tryptophan, though as we have seen the evidence around the exact role of tryptophan is uncertain. Chickpeas, spinach, mushrooms, salmon, and sunflower seeds are all rich in vitamin B$_6$ and you'll find them in many of our recipes, such as *Sun-Dried Tomato Hummus* and *Mushroom-and-Olive-Stuffed Eggplant*.

Avoiding blood sugar lows

My food diary showed that my moments of panic frequently coincided with moments of hunger. This is a bit unusual. Many people I have spoken to say that normally they don't feel hungry when they are anxious. Evolution would suggest that we would empty our stomach in readiness to flee from a lion and eating would be the last thing on our mind.

But for me, the opposite happens. It is an important point. We are all unique when it comes to our response to food. So I have got into the habit of preparing calming snacks ahead. I usually feel nervier in the mornings, so I use my evenings to make snacks if I think the next day is going to be difficult. Preparing ahead calms me. Then I make sure I eat a snack every three hours or so. My panic dissipates when I do so in a most satisfactory way.

Our *Paprika Roasted Butternut Squash Seeds* make for nutritious snacks, breakfast toppings, and salad garnishes. Many of the drinks we have included in this book can also be helpful if you are feeling jittery and in a rush. Inevitably, our busiest times are our most anxious times. I am thinking of Christmas, which leaves me frazzled. Yet the busier we are, the harder it is to manage our diet. This is rather ironic, since it's when we're busy that our body needs healthy nutrients the most.

A green smoothie can be a savior. What goes into your green smoothie is completely dependent on your personal taste (and what's in your fridge), which is why we haven't included a recipe for one in this chapter. I include some leafy green vegetables and banana, which I know contain my friend magnesium, as well as some sunflower seeds for vitamin B and some butternut squash seeds for luck.

Looking after the adrenal glands

I have become mindful of my adrenal glands. These are responsible for secreting hormones such as cortisol when we are stressed, which increases the amount of circulating glucose in the body. There has been a lot of research into the negative health aspects of prolonged high cortisol levels. See our **Nutrition Note** on page 76 for more information. Getting enough sleep and drinking herbal tea may help.

Herbal teas

Sipping a tisane soothes me when I am rattled. For centuries, green tea has been used in Chinese medicine to treat depression. The tea comes from the fresh leaves of the *Camellia sinensis*, which are steamed and then fermented. It is a source of theanine, an amino acid, the building block of protein, which has been studied for its potential role in reducing stress. Drinking green tea (which contains some caffeine) has also been shown in some studies to help improve cognition, attention, and memory.

Chamomile tea has been a favorite of mine ever since I read Beatrix Potter's *The Tale of Peter Rabbit* as a child and wanted to be tucked up with a dose of tea by Mrs. Rabbit. Our *Elderflower and Green Tea Cooler* is another personal favorite, not least because it looks enticing in a tall glass. Be experimental with your herbal teas, and find what works for you. You'll find more information about other types of tea in our **Sweet Dreams** chapter.

Summing up—to help stay nice and calm, I:

nourished a healthy digestive system by reducing the "bad" stuff and boosting the "good"

consumed more magnesium

consumed more vitamin B$_6$

avoided having a blood sugar low by eating regularly, and having a supply of calming snacks

looked after my adrenal glands

sipped calming teas

Nutrition Note: adrenal glands

The adrenal glands are responsible for putting us into fight-or-flight mode—a physiological reflex that maximizes our chances of survival when we are in immediate danger and makes us produce the stress hormone cortisol. This is a good idea if we need to run away from a lion, but unfortunately, nowadays our body often remains in fight-or-flight mode much of the time, and in addition we do not do as much physical work as our ancestors. The cortisol coursing through our body is therefore counterproductive and the nervous energy it gives us has no way of being discharged—particularly if we are sitting still at work, or on a bus in traffic.

When we're under stress, signals are sent to the amygdala, the part of the brain that is responsible for triggering feelings of fear and anxiety. The amygdala then sends messages to the hippocampus, the part of the brain that communicates with the rest of the body to produce that fight-or-flight response. Hippocampal shrinking is a process that has been seen to occur in depression. Gentle exercise, breathing, and meditation are some powerful ways to reduce cortisol levels.

NUTTY SPICED QUINOA COOKED CEREAL

Though this takes a bit longer to cook than oatmeal, it will keep you going well into the day due to the higher protein content of the quinoa. Quinoa has been popular in South America for thousands of years—its name means "the mother of all grains." The crops thrive at high altitude and can grow up to 10 feet tall. The large seed-heads range in color from red and purple to green and yellow. The grains contain magnesium and calming B vitamins.

Our recipe works just as well with cow's milk as with oat milk, almond milk, or coconut milk (ideally use fresh rather than canned). I like to sweeten it with fresh fruit, and recommend mango in particular: it complements the spices. Or choose whatever fruit is in season. The Greek yogurt added at the end helps to thicken the mixture and is a source of "good" bacteria for the gut. Remember to pick out the cloves before you eat it. Despite supporting healthy gut function, they taste horrid when eaten whole.

– Makes 1 portion –

4 Tablespoons quinoa
About 1 cup milk (or dairy-free
   alternative), depending on your
   desired consistency
½ teaspoon ground cinnamon
1 clove (to be picked out before
   serving) or ¼ teaspoon ground cloves
½ teaspoon ground nutmeg
1 Tablespoon seeds or nuts of your choice
1 Tablespoon honey or maple syrup
Dollop of Greek yogurt, to serve

1. Rinse the quinoa in a sieve under the tap and then place it in a saucepan with around ¾ cup milk.

2. Bring it to a boil and then immediately reduce the heat to a gentle simmer for 10 minutes.

3. If all the milk has been soaked up, pour in the rest, and stir in the spices and nuts. Simmer for 5 more minutes or until the grains are cooked. They should still have a little bite without being overly crunchy. You can always give them a little longer and add a dash more milk if needed.

4. Serve the quinoa in a bowl with some honey, maple syrup, or fresh fruit and, to make it extra creamy, a dollop of Greek yogurt.

ELDERFLOWER AND GREEN TEA COOLER

The green tea makes this cooler both calming and refreshing. Be sure to make the ginger pieces thick enough to fish out from your pitcher, and use only a tablespoon of elderflower cordial for every quart of water: it is high in sugar. A tea to give to teenagers facing exams.

– Makes 1 quart –

2 green tea bags
2½ inches gingerroot, sliced
1 quart boiling water (leave it to sit for
  1 minute before adding the tea)
½ cucumber, thinly sliced, or use a peeler
  to make ribbons
1 lime, sliced
1 Tablespoon elderflower cordial
Ice cubes

1. Brew the tea bags and ginger in the water for 5 minutes in a large teapot or glass measuring cup.

2. Remove the tea bags and ginger and let the tea cool for an hour before putting it in the fridge.

3. When you are ready for a drink, add the cucumber, lime, elderflower cordial, and ice before serving.

SUN-DRIED TOMATO HUMMUS
[feeling fragile choice]

I always have a container of hummus in the fridge to use for a snack or to add to a salad. It is rich in vitamin B_6 and magnesium, which, as we have seen, have anxiety-relieving effects, and our version avoids the extra sugar, salt, and vegetable oil of some ready-made varieties. Tahini is a Middle Eastern spread made from toasted sesame seeds. This recipe works equally well with roasted red peppers, and I sometimes switch the chickpeas for lentils or navy beans if I fancy a change. Get experimenting.

– Serves 4–6 –

4 ounces (drained weight) sun-dried
  tomatoes in oil
14 ounces canned chickpeas, drained
Juice of ½ lemon
2 Tablespoons light tahini
2 Tablespoons olive oil
1 teaspoon paprika

1. Let the excess oil drain off the sun-dried tomatoes. I use a paper towel for this.

2. Put all the ingredients in a food processor and blitz until you have a smooth paste. Add a bit more lemon juice or tomato according to taste.

3. Add a little extra olive oil or a splash of water to loosen the hummus if it feels too thick.

4. Serve it with warm pita bread or crudités. Or both!

80

MUSHROOM-AND-OLIVE-STUFFED EGGPLANT

Eggplant is rich in magnesium, and the skin contains lots of fiber, so try to include it in your diet. Any leftovers can be heated up the next day or put in a lunch box.

– Serves 2 –

2 medium eggplants
3 Tablespoons olive oil
1 large red onion, finely chopped
2 garlic cloves
1 ounce fresh parsley, chopped
4 strips of bacon, sliced
10 pitted green olives, halved
1 full Tablespoon capers
1 full Tablespoon sun-dried tomato paste
10 brown or button mushrooms (or any other
  kind), quartered. Button mushrooms will keep
  their shape and not color the other ingredients
  as much as other kinds of mushrooms.
1½ ounces feta cheese
4 ounces arugula, watercress, mâche,
  or spinach salad, dressed with your
  choice of vinaigrette

1. Preheat the oven to 350°F.

2. Cut the eggplants in half and place them skin down on a baking sheet. Using a sharp knife, score the white flesh in a crisscross pattern. You can go quite deep, but be careful not to break through the skin on the other side. Drizzle with some of the olive oil, and bake them in the oven for 20 minutes.

3. Meanwhile, in a frying pan, heat the remaining olive oil and sauté the onion, garlic, and parsley. After 2–3 minutes, when these have softened, add the bacon, olives, capers, tomato paste, and mushrooms. If you use salted bacon, there's no need for any extra salt. Cook for around 8 minutes, stirring often, and then turn off the heat until the eggplants are ready.

4. Remove the eggplants from the oven, but don't turn it off. The flesh should be soft enough to spoon out. If necessary, put them back in the oven for another 5–10 minutes. Scoop out the flesh gently to avoid breaking the skin.

5. Add the eggplant flesh to the mushroom mixture, turn the heat back on, and cook for a further 6-8 minutes.

6. Spoon the mixture into the eggplant skins, crumble the cheese over the top, and return them to the oven for another 15 minutes. When you take them out, the eggplants should be golden brown on top and the skin should be soft enough to cut.

7. Place them on top of a bed of salad leaves and serve.

GUT-LOVING SAUERKRAUT

Warning: your sauerkraut will take five days to ferment. It is worth it, though, since eating pickled or fermented foods is thought to improve gut function, as they act as prebiotics. You can make either basic sauerkraut or the spicy version, which is reminiscent of Korean kimchi. The sauerkraut's sourness comes from the fermentation process, which involves lactic acid. *Sauerkraut* is German for "sour herb" or "sour cabbage."

– Makes 15–20 portions –

1¾ pounds red or white cabbage
½–1 Tablespoon fine sea salt

Optional spices:
1 teaspoon dried chili flakes
2 teaspoons harissa
1 garlic clove, minced
¾ inch gingerroot, minced

Sterilizing jar(s):
Ideally, use a 1-quart mason jar. These jars are designed to preserve food using a rubber ring to create a hermetic seal, but we often use several jam jars. Wash the jars and lids thoroughly. Place them in the oven (separately) at 300°F for 10 minutes. Remove them using an oven mitt and leave them to cool on a heatproof surface. If the mason jar has a rubber lid, then only wash it—DO NOT put the lid in the oven.

1. Wash your hands thoroughly.

2. Finely shred the cabbage. This can be done with a knife, or using a food processor attachment, which will yield smaller pieces.

3. In a large bowl, use your hands to massage the salt into the cabbage. It will begin to soften and produce brine. Keep going until it is wilted and there is a decent amount of brine in the bowl. If there isn't much, add a little more salt, but don't use more than

1 tablespoon or the sauerkraut will be too salty. If you want the spicier version, add the optional ingredients and mix them in thoroughly.

4. Put the cabbage in the jar(s), packing it down tightly with a rolling pin or the back of a large spoon until the brine comes over the top of the cabbage. The aim is to have around ⅛ inch of brine above the top layer.

5. Close the lid tightly (or seal the jar well with plastic wrap) and leave the cabbage to ferment at room temperature for 3–5 days. You can't hurry sauerkraut.

6. You may notice air pockets forming as the cabbage ferments. Every 24 hours, open up the jar and squeeze these out with a spoon. You should see some fine bubbles coming up as you do this.

7. After around 5 days, taste the sauerkraut. You want to try the bits that have been submerged in the brine, rather than the bits on top. Discard any scum that forms on the surface. The regular sauerkraut should be salty, while the spicy one will have more of a kick.

8. Your sauerkraut should live for a year in the fridge if you keep the jar sealed. I like to eat it with cold meat or salads, or even as a snack with some Greek yogurt, which provides a nice antidote to its saltiness, and a few oatcakes.

JEWELED GUACAMOLE AND ROASTED PEPPERS ON RYE BREAD

This recipe brings out the best in the vegetables it contains. The peppers are deliciously sweet and the pomegranates add sparkle to the dish. What's more, they are bursting with vitamin C and rich in fiber, which supports a healthy gut. You can normally find small containers of them in supermarkets, or buy the fruit and scoop out the seeds yourself. I have found it is another practice to do mindfully and with focus as a way of calming myself down. Don't panic if you don't have time or can't get hold of any, though—the dish tastes good without them.

– Serves 1, with leftovers –

2 red, yellow, or orange bell peppers,
  seeded and sliced
2 Tablespoons olive oil
½ ounce fresh flat-leaf parsley, chopped
1 large ripe avocado
½ garlic clove, crushed
Squeeze of lemon juice
3 ounces pomegranate seeds
2 slices of toasted rye bread, with
  added seeds if possible

1. Preheat the oven to 350°F.

2. Place the peppers on a baking sheet and drizzle with the olive oil and a little chopped parsley. Bake for 20 minutes, turning them halfway through. We like them slightly charred on the outside.

3. Scoop out the avocado flesh and mash it together with the garlic and a dash of olive oil. We prefer it a little lumpy, but if you want a smooth consistency, mash away to your heart's content.

4. Add a squeeze of lemon (not too much) and mix in the pomegranate seeds.

5. Once the peppers are cooked, you are ready to serve. Drizzle olive or hempseed oil over the hot toast, and then spread on the guacamole. Place the roasted peppers on top and add a sprinkle of parsley. The guacamole can be stored in the fridge but may go a little brown as the avocado oxidizes, so it is better eaten the same day.

SAFFRON CHICKEN WITH QUINOA AND CAULIFLOWER TABBOULEH

This isn't our speediest dish, but it is definitely worth the effort. The vegetables will help support your gut, while the quinoa will provide slow-release energy. Also, it contains saffron, which as we have seen is thought to alleviate anxiety. If you use a bigger cauliflower, you may have leftover cauliflower "rice," which can be steamed and used to accompany many of our recipes. I wish I'd known sooner in my life that cauliflower could be transformed in this way. Tabbouleh is a Middle Eastern vegetarian dish—we have devised our own version here.

– Serves 3–4 –

For the chicken:
½ teaspoon saffron threads
¼ cup warm water
8 chicken thighs (skin on) or chicken
   breasts if you prefer
1 Tablespoon olive oil
4 garlic cloves, finely chopped
1 teaspoon paprika
1 teaspoon ground cumin
½–1 teaspoon chili powder, to taste

For the tabbouleh:
1 cup uncooked quinoa
½ medium cauliflower
Juice of 1 lemon
4 Tablespoons olive oil
10 fresh mint leaves, roughly chopped
1 ounce fresh parsley, roughly chopped
7–8 ounces cherry tomatoes, finely chopped
½ cucumber, finely diced
½ red onion, finely diced

1. Preheat the oven to 350°F. Add the saffron to the warm water and let it steep for 10 minutes.

2. Marinate the chicken in the oil, garlic, spices, and saffron water for an hour.

3. Place the chicken in a baking dish (don't worry if there is some watery marinade, the chicken will absorb it as it cooks) and bake it for 30–35 minutes. The skin should be nicely crispy on top but not burned.

4. Put the quinoa in a large pan with 1½ cups water (you can add a vegetable stock cube for extra flavor). Bring it to a boil and then turn the heat down and simmer for 8–10 minutes.

5. While the chicken and quinoa are cooking, grate the cauliflower. The quickest way is in a food processor with a grating blade. Otherwise, chop it as fine as possible, or use a grater.

6. When the quinoa has been cooking for 8–10 minutes, place the cauliflower on top to steam. Make sure there is still some water at the bottom of the pan, and add a little if needed. Both should be cooked after 5 minutes.

7. Blend the lemon juice, olive oil, and half the herbs in a bowl. Stir through the quinoa and cauliflower, along with the tomatoes, cucumber, red onion, and the rest of the herbs. Add an extra drizzle of olive oil, if desired, before serving.

CALMING GREEN BROTH

The magnesium in this recipe could be responsible for the calming effect it has on me. You can be flexible with the green vegetables you use. Cauliflower, for example, works as well as broccoli, and you can replace the cavolo nero, which is Italian for "black cabbage," with kale or cabbage. If you can't find a bouquet garni in the market, bundle up any spare bay, rosemary, and thyme with string and make your own.

– Serves 2 –

1 Tablespoon olive oil
1 leek, roughly chopped
1 zucchini, roughly chopped
4 ounces broccoli, roughly chopped
1 ounce fresh parsley, roughly chopped
4 garlic cloves, finely chopped or crushed
2 cups vegetable stock
1 bouquet garni
4 ounces cavolo nero, kale, or spring greens
4 ounces spinach leaves
Pinch of chili flakes (optional)
1 teaspoon tamari (optional)

1. Heat the oil in a large saucepan and sauté the leek, zucchini, and broccoli with the parsley and garlic for 2–3 minutes.

2. Add the stock and bouquet garni.

3. Chop the cavolo nero or greens into strips (the broth won't be blended, so keep them quite small) and add them to the pan too. Don't stir them in— let them sit on top.

4. Cover the pot with a lid, turn the heat down to low, and leave it to simmer for 20–25 minutes.

5. About 4 minutes before the end of cooking time, add the spinach leaves. These will wilt quickly.

6. If you like a little more spice, you can add the tamari and chili flakes. Remember to take out the bouquet garni before serving.

CINNAMON, ALMOND, AND LAMB CURRY WITH CILANTRO BROWN RICE

This recipe is inspired by beef randang, the popular Malaysian dish served on holidays, and although it contains a lot of ingredients, it is actually quite easy to make. Almonds are a source of magnesium, while ginger, chili, turmeric, and garlic all contain antioxidants, and the spices add a lovely depth of flavor to the dish. If you are a vegetarian, try substituting chickpeas for the lamb; they, like the lamb, contain iron, fiber, and B vitamins. Cooking time for the chickpeas—if you go with the dried variety, rather than a can—is around an hour, and you may have to soak them beforehand too. Once all the preparation is out of the way, the dish slow-cooks in the oven without needing any help and can be eaten the next day. The combination of almonds, coconut, and lamb means this dish is relatively high in fat, so I find I only need a small portion.

– Serves 4–6 –

For the curry paste:
2 red onions, roughly chopped
6 garlic cloves
2 lemongrass stalks, white parts only with
  the tough outer layer removed
4 red chilies, seeded (if you like it hot, keep
  the seeds in 2 of the chilies)
1 Tablespoon liquid coconut oil
1 ounce fresh cilantro, finely chopped
2 ounces gingerroot, roughly chopped
½ ounce fresh turmeric (many Asian supermarkets
  sell this) or 2 teaspoons ground turmeric
2 teaspoons ground coriander
1 teaspoon ground cumin
1 Tablespoon maple syrup or palm sugar

For the curry:
4 star anise
2 cinnamon sticks
1¼ pounds leg of lamb (boneless), diced
1 medium-size sweet potato, cut
  into 1½-inch chunks
1¾ cups coconut milk
3 Tablespoons water
1 Tablespoon tamarind paste
4 kaffir lime leaves
Juice and zest of 1 lime
4 ounces raw almonds
¼ cup coconut flakes or dried coconut

For the cilantro rice:
1½ cups brown rice
2½ cups water
4 cardamom pods
1½ ounces fresh cilantro,
  finely chopped

continued on next page

1. Preheat the oven to 300°F.

2. Place all the paste ingredients in a food processor and blend to form a smooth purée, or crush up well using a mortar and pestle.

3. Heat a heavy-based casserole (with a lid) on the stovetop and fry the paste over high heat for 2 minutes.

4. Add the star anise and cinnamon sticks and cook for another minute, then stir the meat into the mixture so that it gets a good coating.

5. Add the sweet potato chunks, coconut milk, water, tamarind paste, kaffir lime leaves, and lime juice and zest, and give it a good stir.

6. Cover with the lid and put the curry in the oven for 1½–2 hours, stirring it halfway through and checking that it isn't cooking too quickly—it should be gently simmering, not boiling.

7. Meanwhile, use the food processor to chop up the almonds. Pulse until they are broken into small pieces.

8. After 2 hours, take the curry out and stir in the almonds and coconut. The meat should already be nice and tender. If the mixture is still quite liquid, you can take the lid off before putting it back into the oven for the last 20 minutes, otherwise leave it on. I recommend giving the dish around 15 minutes to rest before serving, so keep this in mind when cooking the rice. If there is a layer of fat on top of the curry, use a spoon to remove some of it.

9. For the rice, start by rinsing it well in a sieve under the tap. Transfer it to a pan with the water and cardamom pods, bring it to a boil, then reduce the heat and put the lid on. Cook it on gentle heat for 25–30 minutes.

10. You should start to see air bubbles form in the rice where the air is escaping, and at this point most of the water should have gone. Stir in the chopped cilantro, replace the lid, and allow it to steam for 5 minutes with the heat turned off.

11. Fish out the cardamom pods, then serve the rice with the curry on top, doing your best to avoid the cinnamon sticks and star anise. Garnish with some chopped fresh red chili if you like it hot.

PAPRIKA ROASTED BUTTERNUT SQUASH SEEDS

I used to throw the squash seeds away, until I learned that they are a nutritional gold mine because they contain tryptophan, which may help lessen anxiety levels. This recipe uses the seeds of one butternut squash, although I often prepare bigger batches, having saved the seeds from another day.

– Serves 2 –

Seeds of 1 butternut squash (a medium-size squash normally yields about 1½ ounces of seeds)
1 Tablespoon olive oil
½ teaspoon paprika

1. Preheat the oven to 325°F. Spread the seeds on a baking sheet, sprinkle over the olive oil, and roast them for 15–20 minutes.

2. Remove the seeds from the oven and allow them to cool for 30 minutes.

3. The seeds can be eaten whole, but if you find them a bit too fibrous, you can grind them up in a coffee grinder or food processor. The resultant powder is handy to add to salads, snacks, homemade breads, and savory scones, or simply eat it with cottage cheese on oatcakes for a mood-boosting snack.

UPLIFTING SPICED SAFFRON TEA

As discussed in our Golden Rules, saffron has been used in traditional medicine for generations and has been shown in some studies to help alleviate anxiety and improve mood. This tea has an intense aroma and flavor. We use a rooibos tea bag, which is caffeine-free—chai is a nice alternative, though it does contain caffeine. I find drinking the tea from a favorite cup makes all the difference. As Oscar Wilde said, "I adore simple pleasures. They are the last refuge of the complex."

– Serves 1 –

⅔ cup water
1 cinnamon stick, or ½ teaspoon
  ground cinnamon
3 cardamom pods
3 cloves
Pinch of saffron
¾ cup plus 2 Tablespoons almond, oat, or cow's milk
1 rooibos (or chai) tea bag
Pinch of turmeric powder
1 Tablespoon maple syrup or honey

1. Place the water, cinnamon, cardamom, and cloves in a pan and simmer gently for 5 minutes.

2. Turn off the heat, add the saffron, and leave it to steep for 5–10 minutes or longer if you aren't in a rush.

3. Then add the milk, tea bag, and turmeric, and heat gently through without boiling for 1–2 minutes, or longer if you want the tea flavors to be stronger.

4. Remove the tea bag, add the maple syrup, and pour the tea into your favorite cup, glass, or mug. You can strain it first, but I prefer to leave the spices in, avoiding the cloves, cinnamon, and cardamom as I drink but enjoying the odd saffron strand.

NICE AND CALM: ESSENTIAL FOODS

Gut-supporting foods	Fruits and vegetables of all sorts, especially when fermented or pickled, including sauerkraut and Jerusalem artichokes. Other fermented food such as kimchi and kombucha fermented tea, which you can make yourself at home—the ingredients are easy to get online. Yogurt, including plain probiotic, Greek, or coconut yogurt, and kefir, a fermented milk product.
Healthy fats	Oily fish, including salmon and mackerel.
Magnesium	Sunflower seeds, quinoa, oats, brown rice, lentils, almonds, spinach, watercress, broccoli, bananas, avocados, raw cacao, and dark chocolate. Also try Epsom salts for absorption of magnesium through the skin in a warm bath.
Vitamin B$_6$	Beef, chicken, turkey, pork, salmon, tuna, sweet potatoes, chickpeas, lentils, spinach, and sunflower seeds.
Slow-release carbohydrates	Quinoa, whole-grain bread, hummus, brown rice, beans, legumes, oats, sweet potatoes, white potatoes with their skins on, butternut squash seeds, pumpkin seeds, and hempseeds.
Calming teas	Lavender, chamomile, rosemary, lime flower, fresh lemon balm, saffron, and green tea.

NICE AND CALM: MEAL PLANNER

Breakfast	Nutty Spiced Quinoa Cooked Cereal with Greek yogurt 2 tablespoons oat bran with 1 tablespoon natural yogurt and fresh fruit (apples, pears, berries); sprinkle with pumpkin seeds and chopped walnuts.
Morning snack	Sun-Dried Tomato Hummus with crudités Handful of Paprika Roasted Butternut Squash Seeds
Lunch	Jeweled Guacamole and Roasted Peppers on Rye Bread Calming Green Broth Mushroom-and-Olive-Stuffed Eggplant Lightly grilled salmon or another oily fish with brown rice and steamed vegetables—see our **Beating the Blues** chapter for more recipe ideas.
Afternoon snack	Gut-Loving Sauerkraut with oatcakes Handful of Paprika Roasted Butternut Squash Seeds
Dinner	Saffron Chicken with Quinoa and Cauliflower Tabbouleh Cinnamon, Almond, and Lamb Curry with Cilantro Brown Rice
Drinks	Water Chamomile, lemon balm, and licorice teas Elderflower and Green Tea Cooler Uplifting Spiced Saffron Tea

From "Morning Has Broken"

Morning has broken,
Like the first morning,
Blackbird has spoken
Like the first bird;
Praise for the singing,
Praise for the morning,
Praise for them springing
Fresh from the Word.

Eleanor Farjeon

mental clarity

Lack of mental clarity is something that seems to accompany my low moods. I remember one doctor telling me that someone's IQ can drop 30 points when that person is suffering from anxiety. Even if you're not anxious like me, a foggy brain is something that I am sure everyone experiences from time to time—that feeling of going downstairs, standing in the kitchen, and forgetting what you came down for, or being bewildered by a piece of work. This muddled forgetfulness is completely at odds with Eleanor Farjeon's lucid and much-loved poem.

When I feel like my brain is addled, I have found that eggs are one of the best solutions. *Alice's Creamy Scrambled Eggs* are easy, filling, and comforting, and they contain choline, which plays a role in a number of bodily functions, including improving cell structure. Choline may also be important for brain development and cognition and is the subject of a number of studies, though more are needed. While eggs are the best source of choline, it can also be found in liver, pecans, and soybeans.

Hydration

Drinking water, too, helps everything become clearer. I try to drink two quarts a day, and often add a slice of lemon or cucumber, or a sprig of mint, in order to make it feel like less of a chore.

Our body is predominantly made up of water, so it naturally follows that all our organs and tissues need to remain well hydrated to function smoothly. The amount of water you need depends on a number of factors, including the temperature, whether you've exercised, and your age. The easiest way to tell if you are dehydrated is by checking the color of your urine; it should be pale, not dark yellow. Dehydration can lead to headaches and poor concentration. The first step, if I am struggling with a piece or work, is to have a glass of water.

If you find plain water boring, then herbal teas, vegetable juices, soups, and smoothies count. You will find several smoothie recipes in this chapter that have been designed to boost your mental clarity.

I hadn't realized how much fluid I could get from foods that are naturally rich in water. Especially watery foods include carrots, cucumbers, celery, radishes, lettuce, cauliflower, leafy greens, kiwis, watermelons, and grapefruit. Our *Hydrating Fennel Juice* contains lots of vegetables, as well as some coconut water, which provides electrolytes and a smidgen of sugar. Our *Watermelon, Lime, and Mint Smoothie* is refreshing on a hot day, or after exercise.

These drinks are one way to avoid drinking tap water, which contains both fluoride and chlorine. Both are toxic in large amounts—chlorine was used as a poison gas in World War I. Though the levels in tap water are obviously safe, some people prefer not to consume too much or at least to filter it, and I am one of them. While bottled water is chlorine- and fluoride-free, be aware that there is some debate about potentially harmful compounds in plastic bottles, which may leach into the water, especially if left in the sun. A reverse-osmosis water filter could be useful if you are willing and able to pay to have one installed.

As a coffee lover who finds it hard to concentrate until I have had a caffeine fix, I have been pleased to learn that it is not off-limits. Still, I drink it in moderation—like most people, I become jittery if I consume too much.

We should be wary of recent press reports of research suggesting that those who enjoyed coffee seemed to have a lower suicide risk. I was thrilled when I read these articles, thinking I could drink as much coffee as I liked and it might actually cheer me up. The researchers concluded that those who drink more coffee could be benefiting from a range of other protective factors such as a stable home life, a job they enjoy, and a thriving social life. I know that my enjoyment of a cappuccino is as much about sitting in a café with a friend as the coffee itself, not to mention the frothy milk on top and the sprinkle of chocolate. So enjoy instead our *Iced Coffee Smoothie*, a recipe for getting a caffeine hit without the guilt or the sugary extras.

Purple foods

Bright purple foods and berries may clear our mind, and they certainly help me think straight. Their pigment indicates the antioxidants they contain. Some purple foods such as beets may also help the body produce a compound called nitric oxide, which may help to increase blood flow around the body by relaxing blood vessels—see our **Nutrition Note** below. We recommend adding berries of all colors to breakfasts, desserts, and smoothies, or freezing them for a summer snack. Red berries such as strawberries and raspberries also contain good levels of antioxidants. Enjoy our *Blissful Berry Smoothie*; *Cecilia's Purple Risotto with Goat Cheese, Walnuts, and Beets*; and *Strawberry Sorbet*, or try our *Best-Ever Red Cabbage*.

Rosemary and other herbs

Rosemary is traditionally thought to boost memory. It was revered by the ancient Greeks, and scholars wore a wreath made from its branches while sitting exams. Sage may also be useful for teenagers taking exams. It produces oils that are used in aromatherapy and are thought to improve concentration and memory. Ginseng, too, may improve cognitive performance. This plant is grown in many parts of the world, but the Korean species is the one that is most commonly used. It is a powerful stimulant, so it should be used with caution. Siberian ginseng is less stimulatory, so choose that if possible. A word of warning: When I first became interested in nutrition, I believed that herbs and plants were less powerful than man-made

Nutrition Note: berries

Berries contain different kinds of antioxidants, including anthocyanin, which is responsible for dark-purple and red coloring. A number of studies have looked at the effect of certain compounds in blueberries and blackberries on brain function and memory. If you had to choose one berry, the king of Good Mood Food would be the blueberry. Blueberries are a good source of vitamins K and C, as well as fiber, manganese, and antioxidants. Scientists are also investigating whether they help protect against heart disease and some cancers.

drugs. But plant supplements and alternative therapies can be every bit as potent as conventional medicine. Seek specialist advice before taking any supplements—some have potentially strong side effects, especially for pregnant women and children. While I enjoy the benefits of sage and rosemary in aromatherapy oils, I am not one for extra doses of any type of ginseng.

Seafood

Eating more seafood could help with memory loss. In a 2016 study on aging and dementia, the consumption of seafood in elderly participants was associated with a smaller decline in memory and other cognitive functions. This may be due to the presence of omega-3, which is essential for brain development. Another possible factor is an increased intake of zinc, which is found in seafood such as crab, mussels, oysters, fish, and scallops. As we've seen already in the **Beating the Blues** chapter, zinc is something of a nutritional star. Try eating seafood for a couple of weeks. Then try a few simple memory tests.

Crab and other pink and orange seafood such as salmon and shrimp contain astaxanthin, an antioxidant that appears to improve cognitive function when taken as a supplement, according to one small 2012 study. Try our *Easy Crab and Artichoke Dip* if you are cooking or eating crab for the first time. It's simple to make and subtle in flavor.

Exercise

As anyone who has started a piece of work after going for a run knows, exercise helps us think straight. Read our **Nutrition Note** below (even though it is not strictly a nutritional matter) to find out more. And now I am off to my weekly dance class, which, as readers of my earlier book *Walking on Sunshine* will know, is my favorite form of exercise.

Summing up—to help my mental clarity, I:

consumed more choline

made sure I was hydrated

ate more purple foods

used rosemary and other herbs

ate more seafood

exercised

Nutrition Note: exercise, memory, and mood

There have been a number of studies recently looking into how cardiovascular exercise might improve memory. In a 2016 study reported in *Current Biology*, scientists at Radboud University in the Netherlands showed 90 virtual objects to 72 people, asking them to remember their positions. They then split the participants into three groups. One exercised immediately, one exercised after four hours, and one group did no exercise. Two days later, they came back and were tested on the memory task. Those who had exercised four hours after initially seeing the objects outperformed the others by about 8 percent. These findings are supported by Dr. Henriette van Praag's 2016 study with the United States's National Institute on Aging, which found that exercising enough to get the blood pumping might help memory (because it triggers cathepsin B, a protein that supports brain growth). Interestingly, a 2014 meta-analysis looking at 13 different trials found an overall beneficial effect of exercise on depressive symptoms when compared to no treatment. Thus exercise may have an effect on both memory and mood.

ALICE'S CREAMY SCRAMBLED EGGS

Alice has a special trick of adding the yolks last, which might help to preserve more of the all-important choline (which can support brain function). It is easy to get the timings wrong, though, so be careful. Neither of us feels milk is necessary . . . the soft yolks are so creamy. I now regularly have this dish for breakfast with toast and a quarter of an avocado. I like the way it reminds me of Alice.

– Serves 2 –

4 eggs
1 Tablespoon salted butter
Seeded whole wheat or multigrain toast

1. Separate the yolks from the whites of 3 of the eggs but leave the last 1 intact. Be sure to get as much of the white off each yolk as you can.

2. Beat the 3 egg whites and 1 whole egg in a bowl.

3. Over moderate heat, melt the butter in a frying pan and add the egg-white and egg-yolk mixture. Keep stirring with a wooden spoon and you will see it start to cook.

4. After 1½–2 minutes, the whites should be around 70 percent cooked. At this stage, beat another yolk into the mixture. Being careful not to let them overcook, wait until the eggs are almost done before adding the last 2 yolks. Beat them in for around 20 seconds, then remove the pan from the heat. This should give the last yolks enough time to cook partly, but remain slightly runny. Give them a little longer if you prefer a firmer consistency.

5. Serve the eggs on buttered toast.

ICED COFFEE SMOOTHIE

Alice put this recipe together for me, as she knows I am a coffee lover. The addition of banana and peanut butter helps to diminish the amount of cortisol that's released as a result of the caffeine. Add an extra shot if you like your coffee strong. I do.

– Serves 1–2 –

1 shot espresso (3 Tablespoons)
1 ripe banana
¾ –1 cup unsweetened oat milk,
  depending on desired consistency
1 Tablespoon almond or peanut butter
  (unsweetened)
Handful of ice cubes

1. Make one shot of coffee and set it aside to cool.

2. Blend the banana, oat milk, and nut butter in a food processor until smooth.

3. Add the coffee and ice and blitz once more.

BLISSFUL BERRY SMOOTHIE

I find this smoothie boosts my concentration, perhaps because it keeps me hydrated. Don't be deterred by the brown color—this is due to the mix of purple and green. Though not easy on the eye, this smoothie can do much to ease the mind.

– Serves 1 –

½ banana
3 ounces blueberries (can be frozen)
1 ounce kale, thick stalks removed
½ avocado
6 almonds, or 1 teaspoon almond butter
¾ cup unsweetened almond milk (use less or
   more depending on desired consistency)
1 teaspoon goji berries

Pop all the ingredients into a food processor and blend until smooth. This is best enjoyed right away, but it can be kept in the fridge for up to a day as an easy snack or breakfast.

HYDRATING FENNEL JUICE

Vegetables with a high water content, such as the ones in this recipe, help keep you hydrated. You might want to use organic vegetables, which won't contain toxic pesticides. Ideally use unwaxed lemons, too, as fruit producers spray the skins of citrus fruits with a thin layer of wax to protect them and make them shine. While this wax is safe to eat, some prefer to avoid it. If you are not sure whether your lemons are waxed, give them a scrub with a stiff brush and some hot water.

– Serves 1–2 –

½ cucumber
1 fennel bulb, or 2 celery sticks if you
   don't like the aniseed flavor of fennel
1 thumb's worth of gingerroot
½ unwaxed lemon
1 pear
½ cup coconut water

1. Blitz the fruit, vegetables, ginger, and lemon in a blender.

2. Top up with the coconut water.

--

WATERMELON, LIME, AND MINT SMOOTHIE

This is both refreshing and hydrating on a hot day. Add a chunk of ginger for a little spice.

– Serves 2 –

1 pound watermelon
¼ medium cucumber
Juice of 1 lime
10 fresh mint leaves
Handful of ice cubes
½ cup coconut water, if needed

1. Remove the thick rind from the watermelon, and pick out the dark seeds. You can leave the white ones.

2. Put the watermelon in the blender with the cucumber, lime, and mint, and blitz for 1 minute.

3. Blend in the ice until smooth.

4. If you want it thinner, add some coconut water and blend again.

EASY CRAB AND ARTICHOKE DIP
[feeling fragile choice]

If you have a food processor, this dip will take mere seconds to make, so it's a good choice if you're feeling fragile. I enjoy it in a hot whole-grain pita. Try to get a mix of brown and white crabmeat for the most nutritional benefit. The brown meat contains astaxanthin, which as we have seen may help memory and concentration.

– Makes enough for 4 snacks –

4 ounces crabmeat (fresh is best, but
  canned is fine)
4 ounces artichoke hearts, ideally soaked in
  olive oil
½ ounce fresh flat-leaf parsley, chopped
Juice and zest of ¼ lemon
1 Tablespoon Greek yogurt
Dried chili flakes to garnish (optional)

1. Drain most of the excess olive oil from the artichokes, leaving a little to add to the flavor of the dip.

2. Put all the ingredients except the chili flakes in a food processor and blend until smooth.

3. Garnish the dip with chili flakes (if using) and serve it with crudités, warm whole-grain pita bread, or oatcakes.

CECILIA'S PURPLE RISOTTO WITH GOAT CHEESE, WALNUTS, AND BEETS

This recipe was given to us by Cecilia, a friend and an accomplished cook, who helps develop healthy recipes for mothers with small children. You can make it with brown rice, but it takes a little longer and the risotto won't be quite as creamy. If you are cooking the beets from raw, use gloves when peeling them. Beets can boost blood flow to the brain. The walnuts provide omega-3s.

– Serves 2 –

11 ounces beets (raw or cooked)
2 Tablespoons olive oil
1 large onion, finely chopped
3–4 garlic cloves, finely chopped
1 cup risotto (or brown) rice
2½ cups vegetable stock, heated
2 ounces soft goat cheese
4 ounces walnuts, chopped

1. If you are using fresh beets, wash and trim them, but do not peel them. Place them in a large saucepan and completely cover them with water. Bring the water to a boil and then reduce the heat. Put the lid on and simmer until they are just tender. This should take 30–40 minutes depending on their size.

2. Let the beets cool and then peel and dice them. If you are using already cooked beets, simply dice them into small chunks.

3. Heat the oil in a medium saucepan and sauté the onion and garlic until they have softened, then stir in the rice and cook for 2–3 minutes. The grains should go slightly translucent.

4. Add a splash of water to the pan and stir, then turn the heat down and add the hot stock, ladle by ladle, stirring the rice regularly to ensure it doesn't stick—a lovely, soothing process, I find. This is what releases the starch and gives the risotto its creamy consistency.

5. When the stock is almost used up and the rice is cooked—this should take 15–20 minutes—stir the diced beets and half the goat cheese into it. Leave it for about 5 minutes before switching the heat off.

6. Toast the walnuts in a frying pan over moderate heat for 2–4 minutes, tossing them regularly to prevent them from burning.

7. Serve the risotto with a scattering of chopped toasted walnuts, the remaining goat cheese, and a crisp green salad.

MEDITERRANEAN SEAFOOD STEW WITH GARLIC TOAST

This has become one of my "signature" dishes, even though I know it is rather an annoying phrase. But we newly enthusiastic cooks say that sort of thing. I like the zing of the capers and the rich tomato sauce. Knowing that the zinc in the seafood might have an effect on my memory and concentration is an added bonus.

– Serves 2, with leftovers –

For the stew:
1 large red onion, finely sliced
3 garlic cloves, finely sliced
1 Tablespoon olive oil
1 Tablespoon tomato paste
14 ounces canned tomatoes
1 teaspoon capers
1 ounce fresh parsley, roughly chopped
10 pitted green or black olives, halved
⅓ cup white wine
2 bouquets garnis
½ cup fish stock
2 Tablespoons light cream (optional)
4 ounces fresh shrimp
4 scallops (optional)
4 ounces white fish, chopped into
  1¾-inch chunks

For the toast:
2 large whole-grain rolls of your
  choice, sliced in half
4 Tablespoons olive oil
2 garlic cloves

1. In a large, heavy-based pan, sweat the onion and garlic in the olive oil for 5 minutes or until they are soft.

2. Add the tomato paste, tomatoes, capers, parsley, olives, white wine, and bouquets garnis, and cook for a further 5 minutes.

3. Pour in the fish stock and let the mixture simmer with the lid off for 10 minutes. It should thicken nicely. You can let it cool for a while, or store it in the fridge until you are ready to eat. The flavors will intensify overnight.

4. When you are almost ready to eat, heat the stew until it is simmering. If you want it creamy, stir in the cream at this stage.

5. Add the shrimp, scallops, and fish, pushing them down so they are covered by the juices. Bring the stew to a simmer, then put the lid on and turn off the heat, leaving the fish to cook gently for 5 minutes in the heated stew.

6. Meanwhile, prepare the garlic toast by drizzling the bread with oil. Place it on a hot griddle pan or a grill, or under a hot broiler (olive oil side up first), for 2 minutes, and then turn it over so both sides are lightly golden. You can use a toaster, but put the olive oil on afterward if you do. While the pieces of toast are still hot, rub them with the raw garlic cloves.

7. Remove a shrimp from the stew and check if it is cooked. The rest of the fish should be cooked, but simmer for another 2 minutes if you want to be sure. Don't stir the stew too much, as the fish will break up easily.

8. Serve it in bowls with a sprinkle of fresh parsley, and the warm garlic toast on the side.

BEST-EVER RED CABBAGE

Red cabbage is packed with anthocyanin, which, as mentioned earlier, may have a positive effect on mental agility. Have it as part of a roast dinner, or with a sandwich.

– Serves 6–8 as a side dish –

1 medium-size red cabbage, outer leaves and stalk removed (approximately 1¾ pounds)
1 Tablespoon salted butter
2 red onions, cut into small chunks
2 cooking apples, peeled, cored, and grated or cut into small chunks
2 Tablespoons blackberry jam
1 teaspoon ground cinnamon
1 Tablespoon maple syrup
2 Tablespoons cider vinegar
1 glass red wine (optional)

1. Finely shred the red cabbage, removing all the thick stalks first.

2. Heat the butter in a large saucepan and sauté the onions for 2 minutes, then add the cabbage and apples.

3. Cover it with a lid and cook on low heat for 30 minutes.

4. Add the remaining ingredients and cook for a further 30 minutes. Serve immediately.

MISO SEA BASS WITH GREEN TEA RICE (otherwise known as "ochazuke" if you are feeling flamboyant)

Ochazuke is a Japanese dish in which the rice is served in green tea, almost like a broth. There is something rather ceremonial about this recipe, which involves pouring the tea over the rice; be careful not to use too much. As well as being soothing, green tea may help with concentration and memory due to the theanine in its leaves.

– Serves 2 –

1¼ cups brown rice
¾ inch gingerroot, very finely
  chopped or mashed
2–2½ cups water
1 Tablespoon miso paste
2 Tablespoons tamari or soy sauce
2 Tablespoons chili oil
2 sea bass fillets
5 ounces broccolini
1 green tea bag

1. Preheat the oven to 350°F.

2. Rinse the rice under the tap in a sieve, then put it in a saucepan with the ginger and the water and bring it to a boil.*

3. Turn the heat down and let it simmer for approximately 30 minutes. Keep an eye on it, to ensure it isn't boiling too rapidly and isn't sticking.

4. Meanwhile, mix the miso paste with the soy sauce or tamari to form a thick glaze.

5. Drizzle the chili oil over the bottom of a baking dish and then place the sea bass on top.

6. Pour the glaze over the fish, ensuring it is well coated, and bake it in the oven for 15–20 minutes. The glaze should start to blacken around the edges of the dish, but the fish should not burn.

7. About 10 minutes before the end of the rice's cooking time, place the broccolini spears on top of it to steam (you may need to chop them in half to fit them in).

8. Finally, boil the kettle and make 1 small mug of green tea—around ¾–1 cup—letting it steep for 3 minutes.

9. Serve the rice and then pour half a mug of tea over each portion. Place the fish on top.

*Alternatively, you can cook the rice in green tea. To do this, steep a tea bag in 2 cups of hot water for 5 minutes. Remove the tea bag and let the liquid cool for 5 minutes. Add this to the rice in the saucepan instead of water in step 2, and continue to cook as above.

STRAWBERRY SORBET

I sometimes have this for breakfast! I have found that frozen strawberries work best, as you don't need to add any extra ice. Its fuchsia color is probably my favorite thing about this recipe. For added berry bliss, scatter some blueberries or blackberries on top before serving.

– Serves 2 –

5 ounces frozen strawberries
2 Tablespoons Greek yogurt
1 Tablespoon maple syrup

1. Blitz the strawberries, Greek yogurt, and maple syrup in a blender or food processor for about 40 seconds, or until smooth.

2. Taste. If you have used tart strawberries, or want the sorbet sweeter, add a little more maple syrup. Too much can make the sorbet too runny, though, so be careful. Add more yogurt if you want a looser consistency.

3. Eat the sorbet right away, perhaps garnished with a sprig of mint. If you want to save the sorbet for later, pour it into ice cube trays or ramekins and freeze it. Use a knife to loosen the blocks when you are ready to eat them, and blend them in a food processor for 30–60 seconds. Then scoop the sorbet out and serve it immediately.

MENTAL CLARITY: ESSENTIAL FOODS

Choline	Egg yolks, pecans, shrimp, scallops, liver, chicken, and chicken skin.
Hydrating fruits and vegetables	Cucumbers, celery, radishes, spinach, watermelons, fennel, and pears.
Purple foods and berries	Blueberries, raspberries, strawberries, black currants, blackberries, beets, red cabbage, and eggplant.
Herbs and supplements	Rosemary, sage, ginkgo biloba, and ginseng *(to be used in moderation and with the advice of a health-care professional)*.
Seafood	Shrimp, salmon, tuna, herring, mackerel, anchovies, scallops, mussels, squid, oysters, crab, lobster, crayfish, and shrimp.

MENTAL CLARITY: MEAL PLANNER

Breakfast	Alice's Creamy Scrambled Eggs with whole-grain toast. Blissful Berry Smoothie with two oatcakes.
Morning snack	Frozen berries with a handful of raw pecans. Iced Coffee Smoothie
Lunch	Cold cuts of chicken served with leftover Best-Ever Red Cabbage and oatcakes.
Afternoon snack	Easy Crab and Artichoke Dip with cucumber spears.
Dinner	Mediterranean Seafood Stew with Garlic Toast Cecilia's Purple Risotto with Goat Cheese, Walnuts, and Beets Miso Sea Bass with Green Tea Rice
Desserts	Strawberry Sorbet
Drinks	Water infused with fresh cucumber Green tea Hydrating Fennel Juice Watermelon, Lime, and Mint Smoothie

From "If"

If you can force your heart and nerve and sinew
To serve your turn long after they are gone,
And so hold on when there is nothing in you
Except the Will which says to them: "Hold on!"

Rudyard Kipling

hormonal peace

Crippling pain, lethargy, black moods, and an overpowering need for sugar. No, this isn't a punishment taken from a Greek myth; these are symptoms I, and many other women, have faced during menstruation. The poem "If" has always been a favorite of mine. It was something that my mother used to read to me when I was feeling hormonal and unwell as a teenager. As she said, sometimes there's nothing for it but to try to "Hold on." I have turned to Kipling's classic poem in times of trouble ever since; I even coedited a poetry anthology entitled *If: A Treasury of Poems for Almost Every Possibility*.

In my late twenties, I had my first child, Edward, to whom this book is dedicated. While pregnant, I had learned to cope with fluctuating hormones, but, after he was born, there were still many hormonal adjustments to be made. I managed to get back to work as a reporter after Edward was born, but I became depressed after the birth of my second child, overwhelmed by the demands of a busy newsroom and two small children.

Now, at the age of 51, I have had to face new symptoms caused by the onset of menopause, such as palpitations, hot flashes, and my old foe insomnia, to name but a delightful few. For me, hormonal change has been a trigger for anxiety over the years.

Men, too, can suffer from hormonal strife. They experience their own version of menopause—known as andropause—as testosterone levels drop. While the most obvious symptoms are related to libido, many men also experience changes in energy levels, sleep cycles, and mood.

But what are hormones? They are the body's chemical messengers, and are secreted from various glands throughout the body into the bloodstream, which transports them to organs and tissues. We have several different types of hormones: they are responsible for, among other things, reproduction, growth, and, of course, mood.

In women, estrogen and progesterone are both connected to mood. Recent evidence suggests that serotonin might be the means through which estrogen affects mood and behavior. This is because estrogen has been shown to increase the concentration of serotonin receptors in the brain. So we need to keep an eye on our estrogen supplies. Similarly, a sharp drop in progesterone after giving birth has been linked to "baby blues." Those who have struggled with anxiety or depression before childbirth are especially vulnerable.

How then to maintain our hormonal balance?

Supporting the liver

The liver is partly responsible for breaking down and regulating a number of hormones. And, whether we are suffering from painful periods, feeling vulnerable after childbirth, or going through menopause, our livers are important for maintaining the delicate equilibrium of estrogen, progesterone, and testosterone in women, as well as testosterone in men. Consuming too much alcohol or harmful substances, such as drugs or the pollutants found in pesticides, or eating poorly, may compromise how well our livers function.

The best ways to help our livers are to drink less and to stay slim. And we should aim for a diet low in saturated fat, sugar, and salt, and high in fiber. Dark, leafy greens and cruciferous vegetables, in particular kale, spinach, broccoli, cabbage, and cauliflower, are full of nutrients as well as good sources of fiber. Try our recipe for *Baked Paprika Broccoli with Eggplant Dip*. Colorful foods, rich in antioxidants and vitamin C, such as berries, beets, peppers, and avocado, will also help keep your liver healthy.

Though they provoke controversy because no one food provides all the answers, some so-called superfood powders are thought to pep up our livers. Some believe that spirulina and wheatgrass may be effective, but note that they are not recommended during pregnancy and they can cause strong reactions in some individuals. Our *Harmonizing Smoothie* contains a little spirulina; why don't you try it for yourself?

I like to think of this smoothie as my own version of a multivitamin pill since the nutrients can be easily absorbed and assimilated by the body. To me spirulina tastes horrid, which is why Alice kindly masked it with other flavors in the recipe. Don't forget milk thistle, an herb that has long been used as a liver tonic, although this property has not been conclusively proven. Still, I like to rely on milk thistle tea if I have been eating out, or have overindulged at a party.

The B vitamins are important to the liver. Research has suggested that B_{12} and folate are essential to the proper functioning of the liver, and also help maintain our hormones, and therefore our moods. Deficiencies in them may play a role in liver disease, and have also been associated with depression, probably due to their role in the synthesis of neurotransmitters.

Leafy greens such as kale provide folate. See our recipe for *Kale and Butternut Squash Salad*. B_{12} is found in meat, fish, and eggs, another reason we need moderate amounts of protein from animal sources.

If you like a drink, try to limit your alcohol consumption to no more than two small glasses of wine or the equivalent, three or four nights per week with breaks in between. This allows the liver some time to convalesce. Choose red wine over white, as it is thought to contain some health-giving properties. When you are not drinking alcohol, drink soda or sparkling water with lemon, lime, ginger, and spices instead of sugary options or diet sodas—remember our Golden Rule about sweeteners.

While I have found some changes to my diet hard to make, reducing my alcohol consumption hasn't been one of them. I have been a teetotaler for years. I am a pocket-sized five foot two, unlike the statuesque Alice, and have always found that even a smidgen of alcohol goes straight to my head. I like to think my liver is grateful.

Being conscious of cow's milk

Being sensitive to how much cow's milk I drink has helped me when I have felt moody and hormonal. Cows are sometimes milked when pregnant, or just after giving birth, meaning that their milk naturally contains bovine estrogen and other hormones that can affect our own delicate hormonal balance. Many of these are destroyed by pasteurization and homogenization, but we still ingest some when we eat dairy, which isn't something I like to think about too much. Nor do I like to dwell on the fact that cows have four stomachs and we only have one.

In order to avoid becoming too dependent upon dairy products, I try to vary my diet by drinking almond and oat milks—see our recipes in this chapter. When I have time, I make these myself, as they don't contain the preservatives found in supermarket versions.

While we should be cautious about drinking too much cow's milk, making sure I have enough calcium has been helpful in my quest to feel steady as a menopausal woman. There is plenty of evidence for its importance, and edamame, almonds, green leafy vegetables, organic cheese, and natural yogurt are all useful sources of it.

Supporting the thyroid

The thyroid is an important hormonal gland that plays a major role in the metabolism, growth, and maturation of the body. It takes iodine from the foods we eat to make two main hormones, triiodothyronine (T3) and thyroxine (T4). In some parts of the world, iodine deficiency is a common cause of hypothyroidism, but iodine deficiency is uncommon in the UK and the US, and at the moment I don't suffer from it. But many of those I work with who suffer from anxiety tell me they have thyroid problems. If that's the case, eat shellfish and white fish to boost your iodine levels, as well as selenium.

Selenium, an essential trace element, is present in most foods, particularly Brazil nuts, offal, and fish. Although toxic in high doses, in addition to supporting the thyroid it plays an important role in the immune and nervous systems. Try our *Five-Minute Raw Chocolates*, which contain Brazil nuts. But be careful not to eat too many: one or two a day is about right.

Phytoestrogens

Phytoestrogens are also sometimes called dietary estrogens. They are compounds derived from plants and are found in a wide variety of foods, notably soy, flaxseed, and wheat germ. Some scientists believe that phytoestrogens can benefit the health and mood of menopausal women because they gently boost their estrogen supplies.

Several of the recipes in this chapter include unprocessed soybeans, edamame, or flaxseed—the only way to find out if these foods will benefit you is to try eating a moderate amount, around three times a week, and keep a record of how you feel.

Managing stress

Everyone agrees that being relaxed is important for balancing our hormones. Stress can disrupt a normal menstrual cycle, and prolonged exposure to stress can even affect our reproductive function. Spend time with family and friends, practice your hobbies, or binge-watch your favorite TV show. I'm afraid I go for violent ones, since they heighten my sense of gratitude as I luxuriate in the fact that I don't have to run a crystal meth empire or drug cartel. My own favorite ways of relaxing at the moment are getting on my bike, reciting my Kipling, and meditating, but not all at the same time. If your mind is happy, your hormones are more likely to be so too.

Summing up—I found hormonal peace by:

supporting my liver with dark-green vegetables and fiber-rich foods

being conscious of cow's milk

consuming more calcium

managing stress

HARMONIZING SMOOTHIE

Alice designed this smoothie to help me get more greens into my body, and its flavor cleverly masks the taste of the nutrient-packed spirulina. This gloriously green smoothie delivers folate and vitamin B_{12}, alongside the spirulina's amino acids, which are all good for our livers.

– Serves 1 –

1 kiwi fruit
5 ounces pineapple chunks (including
   core but skin removed)
1 ounce spinach leaves
⅔–¾ cup coconut water
1 inch gingerroot, chopped
Juice of ½ lime
½ teaspoon spirulina or chlorella

Put all the ingredients in a food processor and blend until smooth. We recommend starting with ⅔ cup of coconut water, then adding more if you want the smoothie to be thinner.

--

DAIRY-FREE MILKS

I have made an effort to eat fewer dairy products. So, though I am amazed at the variety of dairy-free milks now available in supermarkets, I thought I would try to make a few at home. You can use the milks in this section in several of our recipes. Rather charmingly, some people now refer to these nondairy milks as "mylks," which reminds me of my youngest's homework.

Almond Milk —makes around 2–2½ cups—
Soaking the almonds takes time, but you can use sliced almonds instead if you are in a rush. Almonds are rich in many micronutrients, amino acids, and fats. I sometimes swap them for walnuts (rich in omega-3) and a dash of cinnamon. If you are allergic to nuts, feel free to use pumpkin or sunflower seeds. My children enjoy this with cacao powder—a healthier chocolate milkshake. The precious almond pulp that is left over is useful for cakes, pancakes, nut butter, and cereals. I often freeze it if I don't eat it within a couple of days.

7 ounces almonds
3½–3¾ cups water
1 teaspoon vanilla extract, or use
   the seeds from 1 vanilla bean
1 Tablespoon maple syrup or honey

1. Soak the nuts in a bowl of water for a couple of hours, or longer if you have time. This means they will blend more easily and the nutrients they contain will become more easily digestible.

2. Rinse the nuts and drain them, then put them in a blender with the water and vanilla. There should be around 3 times the volume of water to the amount of nuts.

3. Blend on high speed for 1–2 minutes, or until the mixture is smooth. Taste it and add a little maple syrup if you want sweeter milk.

4. Over a large bowl, strain the mixture through a fine-mesh sieve. The larger particles will remain in the sieve, so press them with a spoon to get as much liquid out as possible. I normally do this twice.

5. You can either leave the milk as it is (it will have a thicker consistency) or strain it through a coarse muslin cloth, thin tea towel, or cheesecloth. (You can buy a proper nut milk bag online if you make this milk often enough. This removes the need for the sieving step.) The smaller sediment will be left behind, and once most of the liquid has drained, I squeeze it to get the remaining nectar out.

6. Keep the milk in an airtight jar or cover it with plastic wrap and store it in the fridge for 3–5 days. Stir it well before use. It can be used with cereal, in soups and smoothies, and to make our saffron tea. Or simply drink it as a snack.

--

Oat Milk —makes around 2–2½ cups—
This is a little bit thicker than almond milk and naturally sweeter, but can be used in the same way with cereal and smoothies and in tea. I use it to make pancakes at weekends. Stir it well before use, as it separates after a few hours.

4 ounces oats
2½ cups water
1 Tablespoon vanilla extract
1 pitted date or 1 Tablespoon maple syrup (optional)

1. In a bowl, soak the oats in water for 20 minutes. This helps to soften them and makes them more digestible.

2. Rinse the oats to remove the sticky liquid that can make the final result a little gloopy and thick.

3. Put the oats in a blender with the water and blend on low speed for 1 minute. If you want thinner milk, add another ¼–½ cup of water.

4. Over a large bowl, strain the mixture through a fine-mesh sieve. The larger particles will remain in the sieve, and you can press them gently with a spoon to speed this along.

5. Discard the residue and sieve again.

6. Rinse the blender and put the milk back in. Blend again for 1 minute. At this stage, add the vanilla extract and, if you want sweeter milk, the date or maple syrup.

7. Sieve one more time and discard the residue.

8. Keep the milk in an airtight jar or cover it with plastic wrap and store it in the fridge for 3–5 days.

FIERY PEA AND EDAMAME DIP

In 400 BC, Hippocrates chose a streamside location for his first hospital so that he could use fresh watercress to treat his patients. A key ingredient in this recipe, watercress contains, gram for gram, more calcium than milk and more vitamin C than oranges. In spite of this, many of us rarely consume it. It also contains folate, which promotes blood cell formation and the proper functioning of the liver and the nervous system—the list of its virtues goes on. You can adjust the amount of yogurt and chili to taste. Alice loves it with extra lemon juice and some zest.

– Serves 4 –

7 ounces frozen edamame
5 ounces fresh or frozen peas
½ teaspoon wasabi or 1 teaspoon
  horseradish sauce
1 green chili, seeded and finely chopped
Juice of 1 lemon
2 ounces watercress
1 ounce fresh flat-leaf parsley, finely
  chopped
3 heaped Tablespoons yogurt
½ Tablespoon olive oil

1. Bring a large pan of water to a boil and simmer the edamame for 2 minutes before adding the peas and cooking for another minute (if using fresh peas, you'll need to cook them for around 8 minutes first).

2. Remove the pan from the heat, drain the vegetables, and immerse them in cold water.

3. Blitz them in a food processor with the remaining ingredients.

4. Drizzle with a little extra olive oil, and the dip is ready to serve.

FIBER-RICH GINGER, CINNAMON, AND APPLE POTS

These can be eaten warm or cold, or added to desserts or breakfasts. Apples are rich in fiber and help encourage regular bowel movements (important—sorry). Granny Smith apples are rather tart, so you might need to add a little maple syrup or honey or a couple of dates, although the raisins provide sweetness and the spices give them a scrumptious flavor.

– Serves 5–6 –

6 cooking apples, such as Granny Smiths
  (though any apples will do)
½ cup water
¼ cup raisins or sultanas
2 teaspoons ground cinnamon
2 cloves
2 inches gingerroot, finely chopped or grated
1 Tablespoon maple syrup or honey (optional)

1. Peel and core half of the apples, then core the other half, leaving the peel on. Chop all the apples into small even-sized pieces.

2. Put all the ingredients in a pan, cover, and cook for about 15 minutes, stirring regularly. You may need to add a little more water.

3. The apples are ready when they are soft and starting to disintegrate. They should be russet brown, thanks to the cinnamon.

4. Spoon the mixture into 5 or 6 ramekins, cover them, and put them in the fridge. Be sure to pick out the cloves before you eat them.

THREE BEAN SALAD

This fresh summer salad contains phytoestrogens, which may help counteract menopausal symptoms, as well as plenty of fiber to support a healthy digestion and liver. It makes for a filling and nutritious lunch.

– Serves 4 –

For the salad:
7 ounces slender green beans, trimmed
4 ounces fava beans (frozen or fresh)
7 ounces edamame, shelled
4 ounces sugar snap peas, trimmed
1 ounce fresh mint leaves, finely chopped
3 Tablespoons pomegranate seeds (optional)

For the dressing:
1 Tablespoon tahini
2 Tablespoons lemon juice
½ cup water
1 teaspoon honey, or more to taste
1 Tablespoon olive oil
1 ounce fresh flat-leaf parsley, finely chopped

1. Bring a large pan of water to a boil and simmer or steam the green beans, fava beans, and edamame for 2 minutes, then add the sugar snap peas and work for another 2 minutes. Remove the beans from the pan and plunge them into a bowl of cold water. This helps them retain their color and nutrients.

2. For the dressing, combine all the ingredients in a jar and shake. If the dressing appears too thick, add a little more olive oil. If you prefer a sweeter dressing, another teaspoon of honey should do the trick.

3. Pour the dressing over the cold beans, top with the fresh chopped mint and, serve. For some crunchy color, stir through some pomegranate seeds.

MISO BROTH WITH MUSHROOMS AND EDAMAME

This soup contains seaweed, a source of iodine, which is essential for the thyroid gland, as well as amino acids and many other beneficial nutrients, but it can be hard to get hold of. Nori, which comes in sheets, is the most widely available and the simplest to use. A type of seaweed called wakame works well, but it needs to be soaked in water for about an hour first, as does other seaweed—check the instructions. Take care not to boil the soup after you have added the miso, as this can take away the beneficial properties of this fermented soybean paste.

– Serves 2 –

1–2 Tablespoons olive oil
1 large leek, finely sliced
2 garlic cloves, finely chopped
1 inch gingerroot, finely chopped
7 ounces mushrooms, sliced (ideally shiitake
  or oyster)
1 ounce fresh cilantro, chopped
3 ounces frozen edamame
1 Tablespoon mirin
1 Tablespoon soy or tamari sauce
1½ cups chicken stock (use 2 stock cubes)
2 Tablespoons brown rice miso paste (or use
  2 sachets, available from larger supermarkets)
2 green onions, finely sliced, to garnish
½ cup thinly sliced dried nori seaweed

1. Heat the olive oil in a large pan and add the leek, garlic, and ginger. Allow them to sweat for about 5 minutes, adding a drop of water if you need to loosen the mixture.

2. Add the mushrooms, cilantro, edamame, mirin, soy sauce, and half of the stock to the pan. Simmer gently for 15–20 minutes.

3. Remove the pan from the heat and add the miso paste. Add more of the stock if you prefer a thinner soup.

4. Serve with a sprinkling of green onions and strips of nori seaweed.

BAKED PAPRIKA BROCCOLI WITH EGGPLANT DIP
[feeling fragile choice]

This dip is so versatile and quick to make. Have it as a snack or light lunch. Dark-green leafy vegetables such as broccoli are a great source of fiber and help support the liver. By baking the broccoli rather than boiling it, you retain more of the nutrients.

– Serves 3 –

2 eggplants
1 large head of broccoli, cut into long
  strips with a few florets on each, or
  10 spears of broccolini
1–2 Tablespoons olive oil
2 teaspoons ground paprika
1 garlic clove, minced
1 ounce fresh flat-leaf parsley,
  finely chopped
Juice of 1 lemon
2 Tablespoons tahini

1. Preheat the oven to 350°F.

2. Bake the whole eggplants in the oven for 20–30 minutes, turning them halfway through. The skin should be dark—this is a sign that the flesh underneath is soft.

3. Remove the eggplants and let them cool.

4. Spread the broccoli in one layer on a baking sheet or dish and drizzle with 1 tablespoon of olive oil and a generous sprinkling of paprika.

5. Bake it for approximately 15 minutes until it is slightly browned and al dente. You want it to remain firm.

6. While the broccoli cooks, start making the dip. Mix the garlic, the rest of the olive oil, parsley, lemon juice, and tahini using a mortar and pestle.

7. Peel the charred skin off the eggplants, scoop the flesh out with a spoon, and put it in a mixing bowl with the dip.

8. Mash everything together with a fork, or blitz it in a food processor or blender for a smoother texture. Serve with the crispy paprika broccoli.

KALE AND BUTTERNUT SQUASH SALAD

Kale normally needs to be cooked to soften it, but this recipe (inspired by *Deliciously Ella*) uses it raw. Kale contains folate, which helps form new blood cells, as well as fiber, which supports a healthy gut. Massaging the leaves with acidic lemon and olive oil softens them, making them more digestible. It is worth spending a couple of minutes doing this—it is rather therapeutic. The salad can be put together a little in advance, but don't add the avocado until the last minute or it will go brown.

– Serves 4 –

For the salad:
½ medium butternut squash (around 1¼–1½
   pounds), seeded and cut into 1½-inch chunks
2 Tablespoons olive oil
1 teaspoon chili flakes
2 Tablespoons sunflower seeds
7 ounces kale leaves, chopped and thick stalks
   removed
1 large ripe avocado, cut into ¼-inch chunks
2 green onions, finely chopped
1½ ounces hard goat cheese or feta cheese,
   chopped into ¾-inch chunks

For the dressing:
3 Tablespoons olive oil
Juice of 2 lemons
1 Tablespoon apple cider vinegar
2 Tablespoons tahini
2 teaspoons tamari or soy sauce
Small pinch of paprika
2 teaspoons maple syrup

1. Preheat the oven to 400°F. Place the butternut squash on a baking sheet, and toss it in the olive oil and chili flakes. Bake it for approximately 15 minutes, or until it is tender.

2. Roast the sunflower seeds in a small pan on the stovetop until they start to color, taking care not to burn them. Remove them from the pan and set aside to cool.

3. To make the dressing, put all the ingredients in a jam jar, put the lid on, and shake it vigorously. Alternatively, you can whisk it in the bottom of the mixing bowl you'll use for the salad.

4. Wash and pat the kale dry, and remove any hard bits of stalk. Put it in a deep mixing bowl. Drizzle the dressing over the kale and massage it in with your hands for a few minutes, a pleasant task to do mindfully and with focus.

5. Once the kale starts to break down and soften (it will have reduced in volume), you can either leave it for an hour to soften further or serve it right away. When you are ready to eat, add the avocado cubes, cooled butternut squash, sunflower seeds, green onions, and goat or feta cheese and mix everything gently together.

SESAME SEARED TUNA WITH CRUNCHY ASIAN SLAW

This homely, nourishing dish is delicious, colorful, and fancy enough to serve to guests. It contains thyroid-supporting iodine as well as fiber. Depending on your taste, you can add a little more mango and avocado, which boost the slaw's nutritional value. The Chinese five-spice powder can be omitted if you aren't too keen on the anise flavor.

– Serves 2 –

For the tuna:
1 garlic clove, finely sliced
2 red chilies, finely sliced
1 inch gingerroot, finely sliced
2 Tablespoons toasted sesame oil
Bunch of fresh cilantro, finely chopped
2 organic tuna steaks
½ ounce cashew nuts
2 Tablespoons mixed sesame seeds (black
  and white look lovely, but use just
  white if easier)
2 green onions, finely sliced

For the slaw (makes enough for leftovers):
½ red cabbage, finely shredded
1 mango, cut into ¾-inch chunks
3 carrots, grated (or cut into ribbons
  if you have a spiralizer)
8–10 radishes, sliced
1 avocado, chopped into ¾-inch chunks
2 ounces fresh cilantro, chopped

For the dressing:
1 red chili, finely chopped
2 Tablespoons soy or tamari sauce
1 Tablespoon maple syrup or honey
3 Tablespoons toasted sesame oil
1 teaspoon Chinese five-spice powder (optional)

Extra cilantro leaves, to serve

1. Mix together the garlic, chili, ginger, 1 tablespoon of sesame oil, and cilantro in a bowl. Add the tuna steaks and let them marinate for at least an hour.

2. Toast the cashews in a pan for 2 minutes or until they are slightly browned, tossing them to ensure they don't burn. Remove them from the pan and set them aside.

3. For the slaw, combine the cabbage, mango, carrots, radishes, avocado, and cilantro in a bowl.

4. Make the dressing by putting all the ingredients in a jar with a lid and shaking it. Pour over the slaw and toss, then let it marinate for up to an hour—it will lose its crunch if you leave it any longer.

5. Sprinkle the sesame seeds on a flat surface and lightly roll the edges of each tuna steak in them.

6. Put 1 tablespoon of sesame oil in a pan over medium heat. Once the pan is hot, add the tuna using tongs and sear each side for roughly 5–7 minutes (depending on how well cooked you like your tuna). Remove it from the pan and set it aside.

7. Slice the tuna and place it on top of the slaw. To serve, sprinkle over the cashews, green onions, and remaining cilantro.

FIVE-MINUTE RAW CHOCOLATES

It is gratifying to be your own Willy Wonka and make these delicious nibbles. Cacao butter and powder can usually be found in health-food shops. Cacao is rich in magnesium, and Brazil nuts are a good source of selenium. These chocolates help reduce my sugar cravings, and are filling, so there's less danger of eating the lot. Keep them in the fridge—they melt more quickly than the ones you buy in a store. Enjoy. Everyone needs a treat when hormones play up.

– Makes 10–15 chocolates –

3½ ounces cacao butter
2–2½ ounces raw cacao powder, depending
   on how strong you like it
2–3 Tablespoons maple syrup or honey
1 Tablespoon liquid coconut oil
5 Brazil nuts, chopped into ⅛-inch pieces

Other requirements: 10 mini cupcake liners
   (paper or silicon) or molds

1. In a pan, melt the cacao butter on very low heat.

2. Stir in the cacao powder, 2 tablespoons of maple syrup, and the coconut oil.

3. Remove the pan from the heat. Add some more maple syrup if needed.

4. Put the Brazil nuts in the cupcake liners and pour in the chocolate mixture to a little below the rim of the liner. Pop the chocolates in the fridge to set.

HORMONAL PEACE: ESSENTIAL FOODS

Colorful vegetables and fruits *to support the liver*	Brussels sprouts, spinach, watercress, romaine lettuce, beets, berries, peppers, red cabbage, cilantro, avocados, and fresh lemon and lime (for juicing).
Fiber-rich foods *to support digestion*	Kale, spinach, broccoli, cabbage, cauliflower, oats, quinoa, brown rice, whole wheat pasta, spelt, beans, legumes, nuts, and seeds, especially milled flaxseeds.
Dairy-free alternatives	Unsweetened almond milk, oat milk, hazelnut milk, coconut milk, and coconut yogurt. Goat's milk and yogurt are alternatives to dairy products from cows—although they also contain lactose and casein (less than cow's milk), they are not as intensively farmed.
Vitamin B$_{12}$ and folate *to support the liver*	B$_{12}$: eggs, fish, meat, and dairy products. Folate: avocado, kale, spinach, beets, zucchini, lentils, asparagus, and kidney beans.
Superfood powders *to support the liver*	Spirulina and wheatgrass.
Iodine *for thyroid health*	Seafood, dairy products, oily fish, and seaweed (nori or wakame)—be mindful that some seaweed is too high in iodine (such as kelp).
Selenium *for thyroid health*	Brazil nuts, rye bread, oats, brown rice, and quinoa.
Calcium *for bone health*	Milk, cheese, yogurt, edamame, almonds, green leafy vegetables, sesame seeds, tofu, whitebait, and sardines.

Nutrition Note: going organic
As a general rule, if you can afford it, buy organic, especially if you are suffering from hormonal imbalance. Xenoestrogens, which are found in pesticides and our environment, may exacerbate it. Organic choices may help reduce our exposure. There's more information at the back of the book about organic food and why it may be more nutritionally beneficial.

HORMONAL PEACE: MEAL PLANNER

Breakfast	Harmonizing Smoothie Fiber-rich Ginger, Cinnamon, and Apple Pots with Nutritiously Nutty Granola from the **Balanced Energy** chapter.
Morning snack	Handful of Brazil nuts Fiery Pea and Edamame Dip
Lunch	Baked Paprika Broccoli with Eggplant Dip Three Bean Salad Miso Broth with Mushrooms and Edamame
Afternoon snack	Half an avocado with olive oil and lemon.
Dinner	Sesame Seared Tuna with Crunchy Asian Slaw
Desserts	Five-Minute Raw Chocolates
Drinks	Dairy-Free Almond or Oat Milk Milk thistle or rose tea

From "Nod"

His are the quiet steeps of dreamland,
The waters of no-more-pain,
His ram's bell rings 'neath an arch of stars,
"Rest, rest, and rest again."

Walter de la Mare

sweet dreams

For me, as for most people, getting a restful night's sleep is closely linked to being calm and happy. I have used many strategies over the years, both to get to and then stay asleep, including learning and reciting peaceful poetry, such as de la Mare's soothing description of Old Nod the shepherd.

Low mood and anxiety trigger insomnia, and vice versa, forming a cycle that is difficult to break. Chronic insomnia was the way my two depressive episodes started, so it is something I have been frightened of in the past. Now I have learned ways of coping with it, and food is chief among them.

Oats

When I am not sleeping well, I like to start the day with oatmeal and almond milk. See our *Overnight Bircher Muesli* recipe: it is easy to make and I seem to sleep well on the days that I eat it. Oats have been known for their calming properties for centuries.

Melatonin

Many of the ingredients in this chapter contain tryptophan, which is involved in the synthesis of melatonin (the sleep hormone), although how this works exactly is unclear—more research is needed. Our melatonin levels naturally increase as we edge toward bedtime because darkness is a trigger for its production. This is why you should avoid electronic, blue-light-emitting devices around bedtime: they can trick your body into thinking it is still daytime, making you feel more alert and less ready for bed.

Few foods contain melatonin itself (goji berries may), so those that are rich in tryptophan, such as bananas, potatoes, almonds, seeds, and whole-grain oats, are your best bet. B vitamins may help. Our recipes for *Ground Korean-Style Turkey in Lettuce Boats* and *Colorful Goat Cheese, Avocado, Beet, and Quinoa Salad* should help the process along. Dessert is easier. Try ending the day with our *Sleepy Peach, Cherry, and Goji Crumble*: it is not overly sweet, and won't make you feel too wired.

Regular meals

I have already established that eating regular meals through the day is essential to maintain blood sugar balance and prevent peaks and troughs. It has also been crucial in my battle to sleep well. As well as ensuring that I don't go to bed hungry and then wake in the night, regular meals provide a steady supply of helpful B vitamins and tryptophan.

If you eat dinner too early, you may wake up in the early hours because you are hungry or your blood sugar is low. Conversely, eating too late is a strain on your digestion, so I generally strike the balance by sitting down to dinner no later than 7:30 p.m. This means I don't generally need to snack on anything again before bed, though sometimes I like a mouthful or two of calming cottage cheese around 10:30 p.m. before I go to sleep.

Eat a balanced dinner of protein, carbohydrate, and fat

Protein takes longer to digest than carbohydrates so it keeps us feeling full. Fats do too—they are the slowest to digest of all the food types. So if you are like me and sometimes wake hungry in the night, it's a good idea to include some protein and fat in your evening meal. Yes! Our *Deliciously Dairy-Free Ginger, Coconut, and Banana Ice Cream* is permitted. You will find the recipe on page 174 in the **Comfort Food** chapter.

The ideal is a balanced dinner that includes meat or fish, as well as carbohydrate, which may help the transport into the brain of tryptophan, which in turn is synthesized into sleep-promoting melatonin.

Our four recipes for filling dinners with a good balance of proteins and carbohydrates are *Warming Sweet Potato and Chickpea Curry, Shrimp and Cashew Egg-Fried Quinoa, Minty Lamb Koftas and Beet Tzatziki* served with whole wheat pita, and *Comforting Basque Chicken with Brown Rice.*

Herbal teas

Herbs have been used for centuries to help relax the body and induce sleep. Though their effects are subtler than those of sleeping tablets, I have found they still have quite an impact. Use the whole plant where possible, as the leaves, flowers, and roots are thought to provide different benefits that complement each other, making them more valuable in combination. Good-quality products generally include these different elements, so it is worth investing in specialty brands for teas, tinctures, and infusions.

The most common herb used as a sleep remedy is valerian. It not only is a muscle relaxant, but also may relieve anxiety and tension due to compounds it contains called valepotriates. I find it makes me sleep much better. Valerian is safe for most people when used short-term, but we do not know whether long-term use could be harmful (pregnant women should avoid all herbs, and herbs should never be given to children before checking with a doctor or qualified health practitioner). To make a tea, use two teaspoons of the dried herb per cup, or a good-quality tea bag in a teapot that will keep the vapors in.

Although there have been no clinical trials confirming its sedative properties, chamomile has been used traditionally for medicinal purposes and may have a calming effect. Chamomile may act on a neurotransmitter or chemical messenger in the brain called GABA that encourages us to feel calm and relaxed. A relaxed body naturally equals a relaxed mind.

Lemon balm, a member of the mint family, is thought to improve mood and reduce anxiety and restlessness. In one study undertaken in 2006 on children with minor sleep disturbances, those who took a combination of valerian and lemon balm reported sleeping better when compared to a placebo group.

Lemon balm grows easily in the garden or on a windowsill in temperate climates. Clip some leaves off and pop them in a cup of boiling water. Enjoy the smell, drink it as a cup of tea, or add it to a bath to benefit from its volatile oils. It is useful, too, for any offspring who are restless and up in the night.

Lavender has been shown to reduce tension and anxiety. I am, as you might have guessed, a nervous traveler and find a small lavender pillow helpful on bumpy journeys. I also drink lavender as a tea—simply add dried flowers to a pot of boiling water. You can also add drops of the essential oil to a bath. Inhaling the lavender scent calmed me down after giving birth, so it is my favorite present to give to a new mother.

Passionflower is often found in herbal sleep remedies but can also be drunk as a tea. Like chamomile, it is thought to act on brain neurotransmitters and have mild sedative properties. I recommend it if you are struggling with pain, anxiety, or worry. Luckily enough, it comes without the resultant "hangover" or woozy feeling often experienced the day after taking sleeping tablets.

Bedtime routine

Finally, for many years now I have had quite a strict bedtime routine, almost as if I were treating myself like a small child. I don't stay up too late, aiming to get to bed by 11 p.m. at the latest. Having a regular bedtime has helped with my insomnia as well as my mood more generally. Having an oat bath, too, is nicely soporific. Add a "tea bag" (3 tablespoons of oats tied up in a muslin cloth, or in the foot of a pair of old stockings) to a hot bath. An Epsom salt bath—find details of how to run one at the end of this chapter—or a drop of essential oil such as lavender or chamomile can make all the difference too.

A proper supper, a cup of herbal tea—be it passionflower and sage or chamomile—and a small snack if needed help keep my blood sugar balanced overnight, meaning I tend not to wake up at ridiculous hours. We created our *Midnight Dip* for those unexpected wakings.

Experiment with some of these suggestions, and let us know what works for you. Sweet dreams.

Summing up—to help myself sleep, I:

ate oats

boosted my melatonin

took regular meals throughout the day

ate a filling dinner with balanced protein, carbohydrate, and fat

drank herbal teas

adhered to a bedtime routine

OVERNIGHT BIRCHER MUESLI

Making a nutritious breakfast doesn't have to be time-consuming: you can prepare this one overnight. We use full-fat yogurt, which contains vitamins D, E, and K. For a dairy-free option, use coconut yogurt. We'd recommend avoiding extra-thick oats (they absorb too much moisture). If the mixture is too thick, add more almond milk. It should last three or four days in an airtight container in the fridge.

– Serves 2 –

3 Tablespoons rolled oats
4 Tablespoons natural yogurt
1 Tablespoon chia seeds
Handful of almonds, chopped
Pinch of ground cinnamon
¼ cup low-fat milk, more if needed
  (or dairy-free alternative such as unsweetened
  almond or oat milk)
3 ounces fresh berries of your choice
1 Tablespoon pumpkin seeds (optional)
1 Tablespoon goji berries (optional)

1. Stir together the oats, yogurt, chia seeds, almonds, cinnamon, and milk. Leave the mixture in the fridge in a covered jar or tub for 4 hours, or overnight. It should form a thick, creamy consistency. Add more milk if you prefer it a little thinner.

2. When you are ready to eat, add the fresh berries and pumpkin seeds. You can also sprinkle over some goji berries if you want extra color and sweetness.

BUTTERNUT SQUASH, SUN-DRIED TOMATO, AND FETA FRITTATA

[feeling fragile choice]

This is another easy recipe that can be prepared in advance. We like it both cold (with a salad for lunch) and warm (for supper). It fills you up, and the feta cheese and seeds included in the recipe contain tryptophan, which is involved in the synthesis of the sleep hormone melatonin.

– Serves 2 –

7 ounces butternut squash, diced into ¾-inch cubes
2 Tablespoons olive oil
6 eggs
4 ounces sun-dried tomatoes, drained and roughly chopped
2 ounces sunflower or pumpkin seeds
2 ounces feta cheese

1. Preheat the oven to 425°F.

2. Put the butternut squash in a roasting dish and sprinkle over 1 tablespoon of the olive oil. Roast it in the oven for about 15 minutes, or until it begins to soften. Remove it from the oven and let it cool.

3. Beat the eggs in a large bowl. Stir in the sun-dried tomatoes, butternut squash, and seeds. Crumble in the feta and then gently mix everything together.

4. Heat the remaining olive oil in an ovenproof pan and pour in the egg mixture. Cook it gently on the stovetop for about 2 minutes or until the eggs start to set.

5. Place the pan in the oven for 8–10 minutes, or until the frittata has puffed up and turned a golden color.

6. Cut it into wedges and serve it with a green salad.

COLORFUL GOAT CHEESE, AVOCADO, BEET, AND QUINOA SALAD

Many recipes use these ingredients, but we hope you will like our version. It contains a good balance of carbohydrates, fats, and protein to stop you waking from hunger in the night.

– Serves 2–4 –

1¾ cups quinoa
3 medium-size cooked beets
2 ripe avocados
4 ounces soft goat cheese with rind
3 Tablespoons pomegranate seeds
1 Tablespoon olive oil
Juice of ¼ lemon

1. Rinse the quinoa thoroughly under the tap in a sieve before putting it in a saucepan with roughly double the quantity of water to quinoa.

2. Bring it to a boil, then turn the heat down and let it simmer gently for 12–15 minutes. At this point most of the water should have been absorbed, so turn off the heat and leave it to steam for 5 minutes with the lid on.

3. Taste the grains to check they are cooked. They should be a little nutty but not overly crunchy or starchy, and translucent in appearance. Let them cool.

4. While the quinoa is cooking, dice the beets into small cubes, similar in size to the pomegranate seeds. This is time-consuming but worth the effort.

5. Finely dice or slice the avocados.

6. Cut the goat cheese into slightly bigger pieces than the beets and avocado.

7. When the quinoa is no longer piping hot, stir through three-quarters of the beets, goat cheese, pomegranate seeds, olive oil, and lemon juice.

8. Serve the salad in a dish or on plates and sprinkle over the remaining ingredients. The avocado is best left until last so it doesn't heat up too much and go soft.

SHRIMP AND CASHEW EGG-FRIED QUINOA

This is another dish that can be ready in 20 minutes, or even less if you have some pre-cooked quinoa. Another well-balanced recipe to keep you full in the wee small hours. It works well with brown rice, so feel free to use that if you have some left over, as long as it isn't more than a day old, since rice can harbor listeria, a harmful bacteria.

– Serves 2, with leftovers –

½ cup uncooked quinoa (or 1½ cups cooked)
3 ounces cashews
1 red onion, finely chopped
3 Tablespoons toasted sesame oil
2 garlic cloves, chopped
½ red chili, seeded and finely chopped,
   or ¼ teaspoon chili flakes (optional)
5 ounces fresh shrimp, shelled
1 Tablespoon soy or tamari sauce
1 teaspoon fish sauce (optional)
2 eggs, beaten
1 ounce fresh cilantro, chopped
1 green onion, finely sliced

1. If you are using uncooked quinoa, rinse it thoroughly under the tap in a sieve before putting it in a pan with roughly double the quantity of water to quinoa.

2. Bring it to a boil, then turn the heat down and let it simmer gently for 12–15 minutes. At this point most of the water should have been absorbed, so turn off the heat and let it steam for 5 minutes with the lid on.

3. Taste the grains to check they are cooked. They should be a little nutty but not overly crunchy or starchy, and translucent in appearance.

4. Toast the cashew nuts in a pan over moderately high heat for about 2 minutes, tossing them regularly to ensure they don't burn. Remove them from the pan and set aside.

5. Fry the onion with 2 tablespoons of the sesame oil in a large pan. After 2 minutes, stir in the garlic. You can add some fresh red chili or chili flakes at this stage if you want it spicy.

6. Let the mixture sweat for 3 minutes on moderate heat. Add a tablespoon of water if it needs some extra moisture.

7. Turn the heat up and add the cooked quinoa to the pan. Keep stirring with a wooden spoon until it is heated through.

8. Then add the raw shrimp, soy sauce, the remaining oil, and the fish sauce and stir for 1 minute, at which point the shrimp should already be going pink.

9. Mix the beaten eggs in, ensuring they are evenly distributed through the mixture. They should take only a minute to cook.

10. Remove the pan from the heat and taste the mixture. Add a little more soy sauce or tamari if needed, before serving it with the cilantro, cashews, and green onions scattered over the top.

COMFORTING BASQUE CHICKEN WITH BROWN RICE

Packed with fiber and vitamins, this nourishing dish is ideal for a cold winter's night. It was inspired by a Delia Smith recipe, which we've adapted to boost its health-giving properties.

– Serves 4 –

4 Tablespoons olive oil
8 chicken thighs (I prefer them on the bone, as they tend to be more flavorsome and tender after slow cooking)
2 red onions, sliced
3 garlic cloves, sliced
1 large red bell pepper, seeded and cut into thin strips
½ teaspoon paprika
1 Tablespoon tomato paste
1 cup chicken stock
⅔ cup red wine
8 sun-dried tomatoes in olive oil, drained on paper towels, then halved
15 black olives
4 handfuls of uncooked brown rice, rinsed and drained
1 orange, cut into 8 segments (with peel)

1. Preheat the oven to 325°F.

2. In a large casserole, heat 3 tablespoons of the oil on the stovetop and add the chicken thighs, skin side down. After 2 minutes, turn them over and sear the other side, then remove them and set aside.

3. Add a little more olive oil to the casserole and gently sauté the onions and garlic until they have softened.

4. Stir in the sliced peppers, paprika, and tomato paste, with a dash of chicken stock if needed, and cook for a further 4 minutes. Pour in the wine, sun-dried tomatoes, and olives and cook for another 2 minutes.

5. Add the rice, place the chicken on top, and pour over the stock. Bring it to a boil.

6. Arrange the orange segments around the casserole, poking them down into the juice, then put the lid on and place the dish in the oven.

7. After 40 minutes of cooking time, baste the chicken thighs and check if there is enough water in the casserole. Add a little more red wine or water if necessary. Let the chicken cook gently without the lid for another 30 minutes.

8. Let it stand for 10 minutes before serving it with steamed greens or a salad.

WARMING SWEET POTATO AND CHICKPEA CURRY

The mix of colors in this dish is enough to make you smile, even before you learn of the goodness packed into it, from magnesium to B vitamins. Using unwaxed, well-washed limes will help reduce your consumption of pesticides. There's a magic moment when you add what seems like a mountain of spinach only to see it vanish into dark green strips in the golden mixture.

– Serves 4–6 –

1 Tablespoon olive oil
1 teaspoon mustard seeds
1 large red onion, finely diced
2 large garlic cloves, finely diced
1 chili, seeded and finely sliced
1¾ inches gingerroot, finely sliced
1 heaping Tablespoon curry powder
1 teaspoon turmeric powder or use
  1¾ inches fresh root if you can find it
14 ounces canned chickpeas, drained
2½ cups coconut milk
2⅓ cups vegetable or chicken stock
1¼ pounds sweet potatoes, diced into
  1¾-inch cubes
12 ounces spinach leaves
Juice of 2 limes
Zest of 1 lime
1 teaspoon chili flakes

1. Heat the olive oil in a large pan and add the mustard seeds, red onion, garlic, fresh chili, and ginger. Cook on medium heat for around 8 minutes. If the onions begin to burn, add a little water.

2. Add the curry powder and turmeric and cook for 2 more minutes.

3. Stir in the chickpeas, coconut milk, and stock, and simmer for roughly 10 minutes before adding the sweet potato. Simmer for 15–20 minutes more with the lid half on, half off.

4. Check the texture. Depending on the desired consistency, you can add more coconut milk, but be careful not to stir it too much, as the sweet potato will break up easily and go mushy.

5. Once the sweet potato is cooked, remove the pan from the heat and gently stir in the spinach with the lime juice, lime zest, and chili flakes.

6. Serve the curry with brown rice and a little mango chutney.

GROUND KOREAN-STYLE TURKEY IN LETTUCE BOATS

Ideally, you should marinate the turkey for 40 minutes, so this isn't our speediest dish. Turkey is lower in saturated fats than pork or beef, and a good source of amino acids, being especially rich in tryptophan. I serve it with brown rice or quinoa, which may aid the absorption of the tryptophan into the brain. Turkey can be quite bland, but the flavors and smells of this dish are wonderful and the lettuce "boats" add a satisfying crunch. It's difficult to know when ground turkey is cooked since, unlike ground beef, it doesn't change color. I check it regularly starting 10 minutes into the cooking time.

– Serves 2 –

3 Tablespoons toasted sesame oil
Large handful of fresh cilantro, chopped
1½ teaspoons Chinese five-spice powder
1 Tablespoon dark soy sauce
1 Tablespoon honey
1 pound ground turkey
1 Tablespoon coconut oil
3 garlic cloves, chopped
1 inch gingerroot, finely chopped
4 ounces mushrooms, finely chopped (use shiitake if you can get them)
1 red chili, finely chopped
4 green onions, finely sliced
1 Tablespoon maple syrup
2 baby Boston or butter lettuces
1 Tablespoon toasted sesame or pumpkin seeds to garnish (optional)
MSG-free hoisin sauce (optional)

1. Mix together the toasted sesame oil, cilantro (setting aside a little for the garnish), Chinese five-spice powder, soy sauce, and honey in a bowl, and marinate the ground turkey in it for at least 40 minutes.

2. About 25 minutes before you are ready to eat, heat the coconut oil in a pan and lightly sauté the garlic, ginger, chopped mushrooms, and chili for 5 minutes, then add the turkey. Cook for 5 minutes, adding a little water if needed, before stirring in the green onions, maple syrup, and a little more sesame oil.

3. Meanwhile, prepare the baby lettuces by removing the outer leaves, giving them a quick rinse, and separating the rest of the leaves. Pat them dry with paper towels.

4. After another 10–15 minutes, check whether the meat is cooked, taste it, and add more soy sauce if desired.

5. Spoon the turkey mixture into the lettuce leaves. Sprinkle over the sesame or pumpkin seeds, a few more chopped green onions, and the rest of the cilantro. You can drizzle a little MSG-free hoisin sauce into the lettuce leaves for extra sweetness, but don't go overboard—it contains sugar. Serve the boats with quinoa or brown rice.

MINTY LAMB KOFTAS WITH BEET TZATZIKI

We haven't included a huge amount of lamb in this book, because it can be quite fatty. It does, however, contain B vitamins, which may help with the production of tryptophan. The purple of the beet tzatziki makes this one of our prettiest dishes. We recommend you follow it with our *Sleepy Peach, Cherry, and Goji Crumble* for a good carbohydrate boost.

– Serves 2 –

For the koftas:
14 ounces ground lamb
1 small onion, finely chopped
2 Tablespoons chili oil, or 1 teaspoon
  chili flakes with 2 Tablespoons olive oil
1 teaspoon ground cumin
1 teaspoon paprika
10 fresh mint leaves, chopped
1 garlic clove
1 teaspoon harissa
6 wooden or metal skewers (optional—
  if using wooden ones, soak them in water
  before use to prevent charring)

For the tzatziki:
½ large cucumber
2 medium cooked beets
1 pound full-fat Greek yogurt
1 garlic clove, finely minced
Juice of ¼ lemon
1 Tablespoon olive oil
10 mint leaves, finely chopped

1. Preheat the oven to 350°F or fire up the broiler or grill.

2. Put all the kofta ingredients in a bowl and, using your hands, mix until they are well combined.

3. Divide the mixture into 6 sausage-shaped portions, around 3 inches long and 1½ inches thick. Put them on the skewers if you are using them.

4. Cook them for 10–15 minutes on high heat, turning them halfway through.

5. Meanwhile, make the tzatziki. Slice the cucumber in half, remove the seeds, and grate it with a hand grater or a food processor attachment, which is obviously quicker though less soothing, I find.

6. Grate the beets. This is normally easier by hand.

7. Mix the yogurt, garlic, lemon juice, oil, and mint together in a large bowl, and stir in the grated cucumber and beets.

8. Serve the koftas and tzatziki with whole wheat pita or flatbread and a little hummus.

MIDNIGHT DIP

Make this in the daytime; otherwise you'll wake everyone up with the blender. Few of us want to start cooking in the small hours, even though this is more a case of assembling a few ingredients. Dairy is comforting and, alongside calming oats, helps to relax a busy mind, while ensuring blood sugar remains stable. The banana and cottage cheese contain tryptophan, the precursor to the sleep hormone melatonin.

– Makes 4 portions –

3 Tablespoons coconut flakes
  (available from health-food stores, or use
  unsweetened dried coconut)
12 ounces cottage cheese
½ banana

1. Toast the coconut flakes in a pan over low heat, stirring occasionally to prevent them from burning.

2. Put the cottage cheese, banana, and coconut in a food processor and blend until smooth.

3. Eat on oatcakes or whole-grain toast.

SLEEPY PEACH, CHERRY, AND GOJI CRUMBLE

This crumble is full of ingredients aimed to induce sleep. It goes well with our *Strawberry Sorbet* or *Deliciously Dairy-Free Ginger, Coconut, and Banana Ice Cream*. Remember to pit the cherries, though, or someone may break a tooth. A bore, maybe—or another soothing, mindful exercise.

– Serves 6–8 –

For the crumble:
6 medium ripe peaches, pitted and
  cut into ¾-inch chunks
8 ounces cherries, halved and pitted
2–3 Tablespoons goji berries
1–2 Tablespoons maple syrup
1 teaspoon pumpkin-pie or mixed spice

For the topping:
8 ounces rolled oats
2 Tablespoons coconut oil
1 teaspoon ground cinnamon
2 Tablespoons maple syrup
10 Brazil nuts, chopped (optional)

1. Preheat the oven to 350°F.

2. Mix the peaches, cherries, and goji berries with the maple syrup and spice. Scatter them across the bottom of a deep soufflé or baking dish.

3. For the topping, mix together the oats, coconut oil, cinnamon, maple syrup, and chopped Brazil nuts, if using, making sure everything is evenly distributed. You do not want the mixture to be too wet, as it will become heavy and stodgy. The idea is to create a crumbly topping.

4. Cover your fruit evenly with the oat mixture (the layer should be 1½–1¾ inches deep), and press it down gently. Bake the crumble in the oven for 35–40 minutes, or until the crust is golden brown.

SWEET DREAMS: USEFUL AIDS

Calming, soporific foods	Oats and dairy products.
Melatonin-containing foods	Sour cherries, CherryActive concentrate (you'll probably have to order this online), and goji berries.
Tryptophan-containing foods	Turkey, dairy products, bananas, potatoes, sweet potatoes, whole-grain oats, and a variety of types of seeds.
Sleepy tea blends*	Valerian, sweet orange, passionflower, and lime flower make soporific combinations. Drink them an hour before bedtime. Try drinking 15 drops of a valerian herbal tincture in water before bed.
Epsom salts and essential oils	Epsom salts: Add 4 handfuls (about 1 cup) to a warm bath and soak in it for 30 minutes, scrubbing your skin to promote circulation. Take care when stepping out of the bath in case you feel light-headed. Wrap yourself in a robe and be sure to drink plenty of water. Oils: Lavender, sweet orange, chamomile, and frankincense oils might help relax you. They certainly relax me. Add a few drops to your bath before bed and let the soothing aromas do their work.

*You should seek a doctor's advice before taking any supplements.

SWEET DREAMS: MEAL PLANNER

Breakfast	Overnight Bircher Muesli with 1 heaping tablespoon pumpkin seeds and a handful of fresh berries.
Morning snack	Handful of Brazil nuts
Lunch	Butternut Squash, Sun-Dried Tomato, and Feta Frittata Minty Lamb Koftas with Beet Tzatziki Colorful Goat Cheese, Avocado, Beet, and Quinoa Salad Ground Korean-Style Turkey in Lettuce Boats
Afternoon snack	Smoothie made with banana, avocado, berries, and a shot of sour-cherry cordial; add some sunflower seeds and natural yogurt and blend until smooth.
Dinner	Shrimp and Cashew Egg-Fried Quinoa Comforting Basque Chicken with Brown Rice Warming Sweet Potato and Chickpea Curry Sleepy Peach, Cherry, and Goji Crumble
Bedtime snack	Midnight Dip Natural unsweetened yogurt. Half a banana with low-fat or whole milk.
Drinks	Valerian tea Passionflower tea Chamomile tea
Middle-of-the-night snack	Midnight Dip with oatcakes.

From "The Old Vicarage, Grantchester"

Say, is there Beauty yet to find?
And Certainty? and Quiet kind?
Deep meadows yet, for to forget
The lies, and truths, and pain? ... oh! yet
Stands the Church clock at ten to three?
And is there honey still for tea?

Rupert Brooke

comfort food

Our last chapter is different from the previous ones, which addressed particular symptoms. Here I share how I have weaned myself off unhealthy treats and replaced them with healthier ones. Whatever aspect of feeling low that you might be battling, the recipes in this chapter are a way of nourishing yourself. I use them to reward my efforts to eat with my mood in mind and think of them as the ultimate happy recipes.

If you feel unwell or flat, or are having a horrid time, you have few enough pleasures and will naturally be drawn to sweet treats. I'll never forget the pleasure of eating a packet of Maltesers (malted milk balls) when I was feeling sorry for myself in the hospital.

Even though I try to eat well, I find it hard to resist comfort foods. When feeling low, I used to reward myself with my childhood favorites, whether it was a thick slice of sponge cake or the bread and honey so brilliantly evoked in Rupert Brooke's most nostalgic poem. I can still see my grandmother, when I'd grazed my knee after crashing my bike, dipping her spoon deep into a pot of honey before spreading it on a thin slice of bread for me. Our **Nutrition Note** below explains why sugar can be so addictive and the possibility that chromium might help, as we have already seen in the **Balanced Energy** chapter.

Substitutions
One answer to reducing my sugar intake and saturated fats has been substitutions. Here's a list of the ones I find most helpful:

Zucchini, kale, parsnip, and **sweet-potato chips** for regular chips—but consume them in moderation, because they contain high levels of fat

Nutrition Note: sugar and dopaminergic pathways
Like cocaine, morphine, and alcohol, sugar is thought to activate the reward and pleasure centers within the brain known as the dopaminergic pathways. The "high" we feel when eating sugary things might help to relieve anxiety temporarily, but too much too often could lead to an addictive desire for another sugar high. In a number of studies, rats demonstrated addictive behavior on an intermittent, excessive-sugar diet, with their sugar intake almost doubling after ten days in some cases.

Cauliflower rice for white rice

Zucchini or butternut squash noodles, or buckwheat noodles for white pasta

Coconut cream for regular cream

Coconut flour, quinoa flour, gram flour made from chickpeas, spelt flour, and buckwheat flour for white flour in baking

Coconut sugar or maple syrup for refined sugar

Dark chocolate or homemade cacao-rich chocolates for milk or white chocolate

Cacao, dates, flaxseed, ground almonds, dried coconut, almond butter for flavor and consistency in baking, instead of white flour, butter, cream, and refined sugar

Unsweetened plain yogurt or coconut yogurt with added fruit for store-bought fruit yogurts or low-fat desserts

Unsalted butter or coconut oil rather than vegetable oil for baking cakes

Choosing more moderate amounts of other forms of sugar, such as dates, coconut sugar, or maple syrup (see our *Chicken Wings with Parsnip Fries and Coleslaw* and *Dark Chocolate Brazil Nut Brownies*) has proved to be one helpful approach, though be warned—your body treats less-refined sugars as sugars nonetheless, so they're best kept to a minimum.

Chromium is another friend worth making if you are drawn to traditional sweet treats. A supplement containing chromium has been shown in one study conducted in 2005 to help with sugar and carbohydrate cravings in people with atypical depression. Chromium can be found in broccoli, bran cereal, barley, oats, sesame seeds, grape juice, wheat germ, egg yolk, green beans, and tomatoes.

I find making desserts in dainty portions like our *Ba-Nutty Pie Pots* stops me from overeating—they are also pleasurable and fun to make. Our *Peanut Butter and Cranberry Protein Balls* are a filling snack that feels simultaneously indulgent and healthy.

Steady blood sugar

A second approach is to try to keep my blood sugar levels steady, as we discussed in our **Balanced Energy** chapter. In turn, this makes me less susceptible to sweet treats. I find that *Sweet Potato and Zucchini Fritters with Poached Eggs* helps me start my day on a high, making me less likely to indulge later on. The beta-carotene (a pigment) in the sweet potato may also serve as a mood booster.

Our *Cacao Chili Con Carne*; *Salmon, Pea, and Sweet Potato Fish Cakes*; and *Chicken Pie* all help keep me going because they are rich in complex carbohydrates, fats, fiber, and micronutrients. They feel like comforting, healthy treats.

Beware of too much wheat and dairy

White flour and dairy products are often present in traditional comfort foods, and they can be hard to digest. Classic comfort foods also tend to contain sugar, yeast, and refined carbohydrates, some of which may disrupt healthy gut bacteria and possibly encourage inflammatory reactions within our digestive system. While it is easy to assume that you are allergic to or intolerant of wheat or dairy if you feel uncomfortable and bloated after indulging, it may be these other ingredients that are to blame.

There are important differences between having an allergy and an intolerance. This is a highly complex area, but in general a food allergy is a potentially serious and usually immediate reaction of the immune system to a certain component of food. Common food allergens include nuts, shellfish, and the proteins found in wheat.

The reasons for food intolerances, however, appear to be more varied. Some intolerances still involve the immune system; others seem to be caused by stress or poor digestive health. Either way, they can cause unpleasant reactions such as bloating. Food intolerances are generally more common than food allergies, and symptoms tend to come on more slowly.

Celiac disease is different again. It is an autoimmune condition in which the immune system reacts to gluten, damaging the lining of the small intestine, which leads to symptoms such as diarrhea, abdominal pain, and weight loss. Many people also experience a dip in mood when they eat gluten. It is estimated that 1 in 130 people in the US suffers from celiac disease. It is important to seek professional advice from your doctor before changing your diet dramatically if you think you might suffer from an allergy or intolerance.

I am not allergic to any foods, nor do I believe I am gluten- or lactose-intolerant. So I haven't cut out these food groups altogether, as I have said earlier. However, I do now watch how much wheat and dairy I consume. Dairy is a source of calcium, and restricting any food group can mean we miss out on nutrients. But there's no doubt my mood improves when I manage to eat less sponge cake—and it's not good trying to kid myself that going for gluten-free cakes and cookies is much better for me. Many gluten-free foods are high in sugar and chemicals.

Psychological shifts

While being careful about what I ate was crucial to overcoming the lure of unhealthy comfort eating, perhaps equally important were some psychological shifts that I made. I have learned to focus on my food. It sounds so simple, but actually it is something I have had to practice. When I sit down to eat, I can make a decision either to treat myself with respect or to sabotage my peace of mind for a short-term pleasure rush. Slowly I have begun to find it easier to choose nourishing foods, which leave me more satisfied more quickly than processed food ever did.

I try not to think about these new choices and habits as being about losing weight, nor that foods are "bad." I have found the more I think of something as banned, the more I am drawn to it. Diets can be restrictive, and often remove the joy from preparing and eating meals. Train yourself to eat well, and often: Good Mood Food is about adding, not taking away. Find substitutes for old favorites—who knows, you might find something new that you truly love. Perhaps our *Dark Chocolate Brazil Nut Brownies* will become as evocative to you as my grandmother's honey and bread is to me.

Summing up—to eat healthy comfort foods, I:

found good substitutes

learned to control my blood sugar

took care not to eat too much wheat or dairy

made some psychological shifts

enjoyed our recipes!

Nutrition Note: gluten, dairy, and comfort eating
Gluten is the main protein found in wheat (including spelt, durum, bulgur, and semolina), as well as in barley, rye, and some oats. It is possible that some people have "gluten sensitivity," or "nonceliac gluten sensitivity," rather than celiac disease or an allergy to wheat. There isn't as much evidence in this area, but it is thought that the protein gliadin might play a role. A small trial in 2014 of people who were thought to have nonceliac gluten sensitivity suggests that gluten might have an effect on depressive symptoms, although the mechanisms through which this might occur are yet to be fully explored.

SWEET POTATO AND ZUCCHINI FRITTERS WITH POACHED EGGS

Eggs supply amino acids, B vitamins, and folate, while the sweet potatoes make this recipe wonderfully filling and there's plenty of fiber in the zucchini. Ensure the oil is sizzling hot before you add the fritters so that they're crispy and golden.

– Serves 2, with leftovers –

5 eggs (2 for poaching)
11–12 ounces sweet potato (approximately 1 large potato), peel on and grated
4 ounces zucchini (approximately ½ zucchini), grated
3 green onions, chopped
1 garlic clove, finely chopped
1 teaspoon ground turmeric
3 Tablespoons flour (ideally whole-grain such as spelt or buckwheat)
2 teaspoons black mustard seeds
2 Tablespoons oil, for frying (enough for approx. 1 teaspoon per fritter)— coconut oil or butter works well
2 Tablespoons sour cream or Greek yogurt, to serve

1. Whisk 3 eggs and combine them with the grated sweet potato, grated zucchini, green onions, garlic, turmeric, flour, and black mustard seeds.

2. Divide the sweet-potato mixture into 6–8 well-compressed patties, around 4 inches across and no more than ¾ inches thick to ensure they cook through properly.

3. Heat 1 teaspoon of coconut oil or butter in a pan and cook the patties for 4 minutes on each side, or until they are dark golden brown.

4. Meanwhile, boil some water in a deep frying pan with a dash of white-wine vinegar. Crack an egg into a cup and then gently add it to the water, using the end of a wooden spoon to guide the white toward the yolk to keep them together. Do the same with the other egg. (You can use an egg poacher instead if you have one.)

5. Put the fritters on a plate, place the eggs on top (having drained the water off first), and serve with a dollop of Greek yogurt or sour cream. For a colorful lunch, add some arugula or sliced avocado.

BA-NUTTY PIE POTS

These are easy to make, and nutritious: the ingredients provide healthy fats, magnesium, B vitamins, selenium, zinc, vitamin C, protein, and fiber—they're very filling, and you'll only need one to feel happy. The cookie base can be prepared in advance, and the tahini (a Middle Eastern spread made from ground sesame seeds) adds an interesting flavor to it. We sometimes use our *Almond and Toasted Pecan Spread* as the base.

– Makes 3–4 pots –

8 oatcakes
2 dates, pitted
2 teaspoons light tahini
1 Tablespoon maple syrup
1 Tablespoon liquid coconut oil
2 ripe bananas
3 Tablespoons almond or peanut butter
1 Tablespoon crème fraîche, or if you are feeling indulgent, whip up some fresh cream

1. To make the base, blitz the oatcakes, dates, tahini, maple syrup, and coconut oil in a food processor. The oatcakes and dates should be completely ground up so you have a moist and slightly sticky crumb mixture.

2. Spoon it into 3–4 small jam jars or ramekins measuring 4–6 inches across. Press the crumbs down until they hold like a cookie-crumb base—it should be around ¾ inches thick.

3. Wipe the food processor clean and blend 1 banana with the almond butter into a thick cream.

4. Spread the nutty banana cream evenly over the cookie bases. The pots can then be placed in the fridge for an hour to set before serving, but do not leave them any longer, as the banana will go brown.

5. When you're ready to serve, spread the crème fraîche or whipped cream over the top. Then slice the second banana and use it to decorate the pots.

PEANUT BUTTER AND CRANBERRY PROTEIN BALLS

These are an alternative to supposedly healthy cereal bars, which are often full of sugar. Though we use sweetened cranberries in this recipe, they are the only source of sugar, and the peanut butter's protein should slow down its release. Nutty flaxseeds, also known as linseeds, come as you might expect from flax, one of the oldest crops in the world. They are rich in dietary fiber, manganese, vitamin B_1, and omega-3. Ground seeds are more digestible and therefore more useful in recipes.

— Makes 12–15 balls —

1 cup rolled oats
2 ounces dried cranberries
1½ ounces ground flaxseed
½ cup plus 2 Tablespoons peanut or almond butter
2 Tablespoons liquid coconut oil
  or olive oil

1. Blitz the oats and cranberries in a food processor until you have a fine powder.

2. Add the flaxseed, peanut or almond butter, and coconut or olive oil and pulse until everything is well combined.

3. Make the balls by rolling tablespoons of the mixture between the palms of your hands. Store them in the fridge.

CHICKEN PIE

Another healthy twist on a familiar favorite. Chicken is rich in protein, as well as zinc and B vitamins, and sweet potatoes are a great source of fiber and beta-carotene. If you prefer white ones, leave the skin on to retain the fiber.

– Serves 2 –

1 pound sweet or white potatoes
5 Tablespoons olive oil
11–12 ounces chicken thighs or breasts
   (skinless and boneless), chopped
   into ¾-inch chunks
1 leek, cut into slices
10 cremini mushrooms, diced
Zest of 1 lemon
2 Tablespoons whole-grain flour
¼ cup water
Juice of ½ lemon
3 Tablespoons crème fraîche
½–1 teaspoon whole-grain mustard

1. Preheat the oven to 350°F.

2. If using white potatoes, leave the skin on and chop them into small chunks. Boil them in a pan of salted water until they are soft. The time will depend on the size of the chunks, but it should take no more than 15–20 minutes.

3. If using sweet potatoes, peel them and chop them into chunks, toss them in 1 tablespoon of the olive oil, and bake them in the oven for 15–20 minutes, or until they are soft (they absorb too much water if they are boiled).

4. In a pan, fry the chicken with the leek in 2 tablespoons of the olive oil for 3 minutes, then add the mushrooms and lemon zest and cook for another 3–5 minutes. The chicken pieces should be around 80 percent cooked by this point.

5. Add the flour to thicken the sauce, stirring for around 2 minutes.

6. Add the water and stir in the lemon juice, crème fraîche, and mustard, then take off the heat.

7. Once the potatoes are cooked, mash them with the remaining olive oil.

8. Spoon the chicken mixture into a small baking dish or 2 individual ramekins, and spread the mashed potatoes over the top.

9. Bake the pie(s) for 10–15 minutes in the oven. If you wish, you can place them under the broiler to brown the potatoes before serving.

CACAO CHILI CON CARNE

This is a variation on the classic chili con carne. The cacao adds a comforting richness while also delivering magnesium, which as we've seen has many health-giving properties. Aromatic cinnamon might help keep those sugar cravings at bay.

– Serves 4 –

Drizzle of olive oil
1 onion, finely chopped
2 garlic cloves, finely chopped
1 Tablespoon tomato paste
1 pound lean ground beef (or chicken
  if you prefer)
2 teaspoons paprika
½ teaspoon chili flakes (or more if
  you like it hot)
1 teaspoon ground cumin
1 teaspoon ground cinnamon
½ cup red wine
1 red bell pepper, seeded and diced
14 ounces canned red kidney beans, drained
14 ounces canned chopped tomatoes
1 Tablespoon maple syrup
1 Tablespoon cacao powder (or
  8 squares of 85% dark chocolate)

1. Heat a drizzle of olive oil in a medium-size pan and sauté the onion and garlic until they have softened.

2. Stir in the tomato paste, beef, paprika, chili flakes, cumin, and cinnamon and cook for a further 5 minutes.

3. Add the red wine, red pepper, kidney beans, and chopped tomatoes, cover the pan with a lid, and simmer for 30 minutes on moderate heat.

4. Stir in the maple syrup and cacao powder or dark chocolate. If necessary, add a little water to loosen the mixture.

5. Simmer gently for at least another 30 minutes, leaving the lid off to allow the sauce to thicken.

6. Serve it with brown rice, quinoa, cauliflower rice, or a baked sweet potato, and some sliced avocado on the side.

CHICKEN WINGS WITH PARSNIP FRIES AND COLESLAW

I have never been a fan of chicken wings, but Alice and my children like them so we decided to include this recipe as a healthy alternative to the fast-food versions.

– Serves 2, with leftovers –

For the chicken wings:
1 heaped teaspoon Chinese five-spice powder
2 Tablespoons maple syrup
2 Tablespoons sesame oil
1 teaspoon soy or tamari sauce
Juice of ½ lime
½ red chili, seeded and finely
  sliced (optional)
8 chicken wings (ideally from the
  butcher, as they are meatier)

For the parsnip chips:
4 parsnips, cut into thin strips (no need
  to peel)
4–5 Tablespoons coconut, olive, or nut oil
¼ teaspoon paprika

For the coleslaw:
2 medium carrots, grated
7–8 ounces red or white cabbage, thinly
  sliced or grated
1 Royal Gala apple, peeled, cored, and
  grated (we find this is the best variety,
  but any will do)
2–3 Tablespoons crème fraîche
1–2 Tablespoons mayonnaise
Squeeze of lemon juice
1 teaspoon whole-grain mustard
2 Tablespoons fresh cilantro, finely
  chopped, to serve
2 green onions, finely sliced, to serve

1. An hour or so before you eat, mix the Chinese five-spice powder, maple syrup, sesame oil, soy or tamari sauce, lime juice, and chili, if using, in a mixing bowl, then add the chicken wings and marinate them for 40 minutes.

2. Preheat the oven to 350°F. Put the wings on a wire rack in a pan on the top shelf of the oven and bake them for 45–50 minutes, turning them halfway through and basting with leftover marinade.

3. Place the parsnip fries on a large baking sheet and toss them in the oil and paprika, ensuring they all get a good coating. Put them in the oven 15 minutes after the chicken. They will take around 30 minutes. Remember to turn them halfway through.

4. Meanwhile, make the coleslaw by mixing all the ingredients from the carrots through the mustard in a bowl. Start with 2 tablespoons of crème fraîche and 1 tablespoon of mayonnaise, adding more to taste. You can make the coleslaw the night before—the vegetables will soften in the creamy sauce.

5. The wings are done when they are crispy and golden; let them stand for 5 minutes when you remove them from the oven. Give the parsnips another 5 minutes in the oven to crisp up if necessary.

6. Serve the wings with a sprinkle of fresh cilantro and green onion, the parsnip chips, and a big spoonful of the creamy coleslaw. Make sure you have napkins for sticky fingers.

SALMON, PEA, AND SWEET POTATO FISH CAKES

These fish cakes are a hit with my family. Not only do they make a filling lunch or dinner, they are also packed with goodness. The first time I made them, I forgot to mash the peas, but I rather liked them whole: they were like tiny green gems. Making the patties is soothing; setting your mind to an activity helps with anxiety. Don't fret if the fish cakes seem a little sticky—dusting your hands with flour will make them easier to handle.

– Serves 2 –

11–12 ounces sweet potatoes, peeled and
  cut into large chunks
1 Tablespoon olive oil
7 ounces salmon fillets
5 ounces fresh or frozen peas
1 red chili, seeded and finely sliced
10 fresh mint leaves, chopped
1 ounce fresh parsley, chopped
Juice of 1 lemon
1 egg, beaten
1 Tablespoon whole wheat or other whole-grain
  flour, and an extra tablespoon for sprinkling
  over the cakes before you cook them
1 Tablespoon coconut oil for cooking

1. Preheat the oven to 350°F.

2. Put the sweet potatoes on a baking sheet, toss them in the olive oil, and roast them until they are soft. This should take 15–20 minutes.

3. Meanwhile, steam the salmon, either in a steamer or in a colander placed over a pan of boiling water, for roughly 10 minutes.

4. Boil or steam the peas until they are soft.

5. Mash the sweet potatoes in a bowl with the chili, mint, peas, parsley, and lemon juice.

6. Remove any skin from the salmon and finely flake it into the potato mixture with the beaten egg and 1 tablespoon of flour.

7. When everything is well combined, sprinkle a little flour onto a work surface, divide the mixture into four, and shape it into patties.

8. Heat the coconut oil in a large frying pan and fry the fish cakes over high heat for roughly 4 minutes on each side.

9. I like this alongside a green salad dressed with 4 tablespoons of olive oil, 2 teaspoons of horseradish sauce, the juice of 1 lemon, and 1 tablespoon of balsamic vinegar.

DELICIOUSLY DAIRY-FREE GINGER, COCONUT, AND BANANA ICE CREAM

To make this, you'll need to plan ahead, as it works best when some of the ingredients have been frozen overnight. If you like, you could add some frozen strawberries to make the ice cream a delightful pink. Coconut cream is similar to coconut milk but contains less water. It is dairy-free, which is helpful if you are trying to reduce the amount of dairy you eat, and is widely available in supermarkets.

– Serves 4–6 –

⅔ cup coconut cream

11–12 ounces ripe bananas (around 4 medium bananas)

6 pieces of crystallized ginger

1 teaspoon vanilla extract

2 ounces pecans, chopped

1 Tablespoon dairy-free coconut yogurt (optional)

1 Tablespoon maple syrup or honey (optional)

1. The night before, empty the can of coconut cream into a bowl and put it in the fridge to harden. In the morning, there should be a thick layer of cream on top, with some liquid as well.

2. Slice the bananas and freeze them overnight. Don't make the pieces too big, as they can be hard to break up.

3. Put half the frozen banana along with the ginger, vanilla, and coconut cream in a food processor. Pulse at first to break the fruit up gently, then blend until most of it has been broken down and you have a frozen paste.

4. Add the pecans and the rest of the banana in 3 additions, stopping when you reach the right consistency. By now the mixture should be nice and thick but, if necessary, you can add a little dairy-free coconut yogurt to loosen it up. Don't add too much—the mixture can go to liquid easily.

5. Taste it and add a little maple syrup or honey if you want it sweeter, although this isn't usually necessary given the sweetness from the crystallized ginger and banana.

6. The ice cream is best eaten there and then, but if you want a firmer consistency, transfer it to small ramekins and put it in the freezer for 2 hours. When you are ready to eat, serve it straight from the freezer. It should be soft enough to scoop out with a spoon. You can also put the mixture into ice pop molds and freeze it for around 4 hours.

DARK CHOCOLATE BRAZIL NUT BROWNIES
[feeling fragile choice]

We spent ages perfecting these, ensuring that they were soft, rich, and gooey in the center. Though they are still a treat, you have more control over the ingredients when you are making them yourself. Spelt flour is whole-grain, meaning that it won't lead to a sugar spike as white flour does, and Brazil nuts contain selenium, which, as we have seen, plays an important role in the immune system. Cacao is a rich source of magnesium and antioxidants.

– Makes about 15 squares –

10 Brazil nuts
4 ounces dark chocolate (ideally 100% cocoa, or use 85%)
½ cup almond milk
⅔ cup coconut oil, plus extra for greasing the pan
1 cup maple syrup
Seeds from ½ vanilla bean or 1 Tablespoon vanilla extract
2 ounces raw cacao powder, sifted
3 eggs
¾ cup plus 1 Tablespoon spelt flour
1 teaspoon baking powder

1. Preheat the oven to 375°F. Grease a 12 x 8-inch brownie pan and line it with parchment paper. Leave the paper sticking up at the sides to make it easier to lift the brownies out when they are cooked.

2. Roast the Brazil nuts in the oven for 15 minutes, turning them once halfway through. They should be slightly browned. Let them cool, and then chop them coarsely.

3. Put the chocolate, almond milk, coconut oil, maple syrup, and vanilla seeds or extract in a saucepan over very gentle heat, stirring regularly, until everything has melted and you have a rich, glossy-looking batter.

4. Remove the pan from the heat and whisk in the cacao powder.

5. Allow the mixture to cool for 10–15 minutes, and then beat in the eggs. Add the flour, baking powder, and chopped Brazil nuts.

6. Pour the mixture into the prepared pan and bake it in the oven for about 12 minutes. Insert a toothpick; it should come out with a little chocolate residue. If you like your brownies less gooey, put the pan back in the oven for 3–5 minutes, but take it out before the top starts to crack, otherwise the consistency will be more like cake.

7. Remove the pan from the oven and use the baking paper to help you slide the whole brownie onto a cooling rack. Cut it into squares once it has cooled completely.

A reminder of our substitutions	Cauliflower rice for regular rice. Coconut cream for regular cream. Coconut flour, quinoa flour, spelt flour, and buckwheat flour for white flour in baking. Maple syrup or honey for refined sugar. Dark chocolate or homemade cacao-rich chocolates for milk/white chocolate. Cacao, dates, dried coconut, and almond butter in baking for flavor, instead of white flour, butter, cream, and refined sugar. Unsweetened natural yogurt or coconut yogurt with added fruit instead of store-bought fruit yogurts.
Chromium-rich foods	Barley, oats, green beans, sesame seeds, broccoli, bran cereal, wheat germ, egg yolk, tomatoes, and grape juice.

COMFORT FOOD: MEAL PLANNER

Breakfast	Sweet Potato and Zucchini Fritters with Poached Eggs
Morning snack	Hummus or guacamole with crudités.
Lunch	Salmon, Pea, and Sweet Potato Fish Cakes Chicken Pie
Afternoon snack	Peanut Butter and Cranberry Protein Balls
Dinner	Chicken Wings with Parsnip Fries and Coleslaw Cacao Chili Con Carne
Dessert	Deliciously Dairy-Free Ginger, Coconut, and Banana Ice Cream Ba-Nutty Pie Pots Dark Chocolate Brazil Nut Brownies
Drinks	Uplifting Spiced Saffron Tea (see page 94) Calming chamomile tea

NOTES FOR A *happy* kitchen

I'm a wife and mother of five, so my kitchen has never been short of noise or mess. But in the past it often lacked that feel-good factor.

Today my kitchen is a much more joyful place, thanks in no small part to the strategies listed here. **The Good Mood Food Index** reminds me of the best mood-boosting ingredients. It enjoys pride of place on my fridge alongside the **Seasonal Eating Chart**, which helps me buy the freshest produce every month.

Another practical step has been to change the contents of my cupboards. The **Kitchen Essentials** section lists the pantry basics to make your life easier and recipes tastier. It's taken time, but now I know what I really need and the ingredients that are unfailingly useful.

A couple of years ago I also painted our pale-green kitchen a bright fuchsia pink, which makes it difficult for anyone to feel blue.

Mindful eating techniques have transformed my relationship with food as well. They've helped me slow down and savor meals, so I've included a guide to some of my favorites. How we think about food is at least as important as what we choose to eat. Healthier eating should be a pleasure in and for every sense, not a penance.

All these steps are part of a holistic approach to food and cooking, which is about more than just the right ingredients. I feel much happier in my kitchen now. I hope the steps in this section will make you feel happier in yours.

THE GOOD MOOD FOOD INDEX

Our Good Mood Food Index is a rough-and-ready list that divides foods into five categories, identifying those that we should try to eat regularly to boost our mood and the ones that we should try to avoid. The index is intended to be a useful aid. Remember our Golden Rule: variety is key.

You should try to mix and match our Fab Mood Foods with our Very Good Mood Foods and Good Mood Foods as much as possible. Feel free to add your own discoveries to this list.

FAB MOOD FOODS

These boost the mood in multiple ways. We recommend eating some of them every day.

Arugula
Avocados
Blueberries
Cavolo nero (black kale)
Chamomile tea
Crabmeat (brown & white)
Eggs
Flaxseed—*in moderation*
Goji berries
Green tea
Hempseed—*in moderation*
Kale
Kefir
Kimchi
Lentils (all types)
Mackerel
Marmite
Mushrooms
Natural organic yogurt
Oatcakes
Oats
Pecans—*in moderation*
Pumpkin seeds—*in moderation*
Quinoa
Raw cacao powder
Saffron
Salmon
Sauerkraut
Shrimp
Spinach
Sweet potatoes
Tuna
Turmeric
Walnuts—*in moderation*
Watercress

VERY GOOD MOOD FOODS

These don't score quite as high as our Fab Mood Foods but will still help your mood.

Almonds—*in moderation*
Bananas
Beets
Brazil nuts
Broccoli
Brown rice
Butternut squash
Cherries
Chia seeds—*in moderation*
Chicken (with skin)
Chickpeas
Chilies
Cinnamon
Dark chocolate, minimum 70% cocoa solids—*in moderation*
Edamame
Olive oil
Peppers (all colors)
Raspberries
Red cabbage
Rye bread
Seaweed
Strawberries

GOOD MOOD FOODS
Our Good Mood Foods are also our friends in times of need, beneficial for our happiness.

Beef (lean cuts)
Buckwheat flour
Canned fish—*refer to our advice on types and quantities in the Golden Rules*
Cashews—*in moderation*
Cayenne pepper
Chicken livers
Cilantro, mint, parsley, and other fresh herbs
Coconut (fresh)
Eggplant
Fava beans
Ginger
Goat cheese
Granola (homemade)
Lemons
Miso
Peas
Spelt pasta
Sugar snap peas
Tahini
Tomatoes (canned or fresh)
Whole-grain flour (or spelt)
Whole-grain pasta
Zucchini

TREATS
Eat these foods on special occasions, such as birthdays and evenings out, in small portion sizes and with focus.

Alcohol
Black tea—*2 cups a day is adequate; don't add sugar*
Butter
Cheesy pasta dishes
Coffee—*2 cups a day is adequate; don't add sugar*
Cookies
Cream
Desserts
Dried fruit
Fruit juices
Fruit smoothies (store bought)
Maple syrup
Mayonnaise and other creamy dressings
Milk and white chocolate
Packaged sandwiches
Peanuts
Pork (especially fatty cuts)
Potato chips and other similar snacks
Sauces in jars (pasta sauce and similar)
Sausages and bacon
Sunflower oil
White bread and bread products (including bagels, croissants, white crackers)
White refined grains (pasta, rice, couscous)

LOW MOOD FOODS
Try to avoid these foods and ingredients. It may take a while, but persevere—your brain and body will thank you.

Canned soups—*some are fine but check for additives, preservatives, sugar, etc.*
Cereal bars
Diet drinks
Energy drinks
Food colorings
Low-fat "diet" snacks
Margarine
MSG (and other food additives)
Pastries, sweet baked goods (doughnuts, croissants, cookies)
Prepared meals
Refined white sugar
Sweetened and processed breakfast cereals—*check the ingredients for added sugar and avoid anything processed, choosing whole grains where possible. Some less-processed cereals are fine, often fortified and a source of iron and B vitamins*
Sweet fizzy drinks
Take-out meals—*be careful. There are some pretty healthy ones now, though, which take care to use fresh ingredients*
Wafer-thin ham and similar processed meats

MINDFUL EATING

I used to bolt down my food and treat mealtimes as a means to an end, rather than an end in itself. Our digestive system expects us to chew and swallow our food properly, giving the stomach time to prepare the right digestive juices. Up to 40 chews is thought to be about the right number for tough meat and vegetables. Yet the reduction in the size of the average human jaw and the prevalence of compacted wisdom teeth could be a sign of how rarely we now use our chewing powers. I certainly didn't, and even now struggle to get to 40 chews. Even chewing for half that number of times dramatically slows down how fast I eat and has become a bit of a game at family meals.

Eating slowly forces us to eat more mindfully. Our understanding of connections between mindfulness and food is growing (the popular app Headspace now runs an online course in mindful eating). For me, learning to eat mindfully has not been about trying to lose weight, but instead has helped me change the way I think about food. I am now more aware of the food I am eating, and its effect on my mood. Learning to eat a raisin very, very slowly has been a way to eat more consciously. It has helped me be more disciplined and focused too.

Cooking now feels like an extension of my normal meditation routine. I can lose myself in the process. Standing still at the stove, preparing food, grounds me. I become rooted in the moment, and stop worrying. Even on days when my mood is fragile, the achievement of chopping an onion or slicing an avocado makes me feel that little bit better. It is as much about the warm atmosphere in my kitchen as the cooking itself.

There may even be some evidence that cultivating a happy kitchen can help us live longer. For years, scientists have pondered the so-called French paradox. Why is the mortality rate from heart disease in France less than a third of that in the UK? Why do the French on average live four years longer than Americans, despite eating, on average, more saturated fat? One explanation could be that the French enjoyment of cooking and food and a culture that celebrates eating slowly, outside, surrounded by family has a positive effect on mood. The French eat mindfully without having to learn how to do so. For the rest of us, the classic mindful exercise on the opposite page might help.

Eating One Raisin: A taste of mindfulness*

Holding. First, take a raisin and hold it in the palm of your hand or between your finger and thumb. Focusing on it, imagine that you've dropped in from space and have never seen a raisin before.

Seeing. Take time to see it. Gaze at the raisin with care. Let your eyes explore it, examining how it catches the light, the darker colors, any patterns or unique features.

Touching. Turn the raisin between your fingers, exploring its texture. Try it with your eyes closed.

Smelling. Hold the raisin beneath your nose and, with each inhalation, drink in any smell that may arise, noticing, as you do this, anything interesting that may be happening in your mouth or stomach.

Placing. Now slowly bring the raisin up to your lips, noticing the movement of your arms and then your hands. Taste the raisin, but don't bite into it yet.

Tasting. When you are ready, have a bite. How does your mouth move? How does the raisin taste? How does it feel? How does it change?

Swallowing. Do you experience the intention to swallow before you follow through? See what that feels like.

Following. Finally, see if you can feel the raisin moving down to your stomach. How does your body feel? How does your mind feel? Think about how using this kind of mindful eating might change how you consume food at home, in the office, with others, or alone.

*With thanks to Mark Williams, John Teasdale, Zindel Segal, and Jon Kabat-Zinn and their useful book *The Mindful Way Through Depression: Freeing Yourself from Chronic Unhappiness* (New York: Guilford Press, 2007).

SEASONAL EATING

One of my Golden Rules is to try to eat as many different foods as possible. Buying according to what is in season is a good way to have a more varied diet—for example, apples and blackberries after the harvest festival in October, roots and cabbages in winter, asparagus in spring, and strawberries in summer. Of course, while I prefer letting nature's rhythms inspire my kitchen, bringing nutritional variety as the seasons wax and wane, finding seasonal ingredients is not always easy. This list has helped me at least to know what foods I *should* be aiming to buy when.

SEASONAL PRODUCE: SPRING

FRUIT	Apricots Blood oranges Elderflower Mangoes Rhubarb (forced)		

VEGETABLES	Artichokes
	Arugula
	Asparagus
	Cauliflower
	Celery
	Chicory
	Fava beans
		Green onions
		Leeks
		Morels
		New potatoes
		New season &
		  wild-leaf garlic
		Peas
			Purple sprouting
			  broccoli (check
			  at farmer's markets
			  and specialty
			  grocers)
			Radishes
			Spinach

HERBS	Basil Bay Chervil Chives Cilantro Dill Flat-leaf parsley	Marjoram Oregano Rosemary Tarragon Thyme	
FISH	Crab Haddock Mackerel Pollock Scallops Sea bass	Sea trout Turbot Whiting Wild salmon	
MEAT	More mature lamb Spring lamb		

SEASONAL PRODUCE: SUMMER

FRUIT

Apricots	Peaches
Blueberries	Plums
Cherries	Raspberries
Gooseberries	Strawberries
Grapes	
Melons	
Nectarines	

VEGETABLES

Arugula	Fava beans	Tomatoes
Asparagus	Green beans	Zucchini
Bell peppers	Green onions	
Chard	Peas	
Cranberry beans	Potatoes	
Cucumbers	Radishes	
Eggplant	Sweet corn	

HERBS

Basil	Marjoram
Bay	Mint
Chervil	Oregano
Chives	Sage
Cilantro	
Dill	
Flat-leaf parsley	

FISH

Crab	Sea bass
Haddock	Whiting
Mackerel	
Plaice	
Pollock	
Salmon	
Sardines	

MEAT

Veal

SEASONAL PRODUCE: AUTUMN

FRUIT		
Apples	Grapes	
Blackberries	Melons	
Blueberries	Pears	
Clementines	Quinces	
Cranberries		
Damson plums		
Figs		

VEGETABLES			
Arugula	Celeriac	Kale	Radishes
Brussels sprouts	Celery	Leeks	Rutabagas
Butternut squash	Chanterelles	Onions	Tomatoes
Cabbage	Eggplant	Parsnips	Truffles
Carrots	Fennel	Peppers	Turnips
Cavolo nero	Jerusalem	Potatoes	Wild mushrooms
(black kale)	artichokes	Pumpkins	Zucchini

HERBS	
Basil	Rosemary
Bay	Sage
Chives	Thyme
Flat-leaf parsley	
Marjoram	
Mint	
Oregano	

FISH	
Clams	Pollock
Crab	Sardines
Haddock	Turbot
Halibut	Whiting
Mackerel	
Mussels	
Oysters	

MEAT

Feathered game
Turkey
Venison

NUTS

Chestnuts
Pecans
Walnuts

SEASONAL PRODUCE: WINTER

FRUIT

Blood oranges
Clementines
Cranberries
Pomegranates
Quinces
Rhubarb (forced)

VEGETABLES

Artichokes	Celeriac	Onions	Turnips
Broccoli	Celery	Parsnips	Watercress
Brussels sprouts	Chicory	Potatoes	
Butternut squash	Jerusalem	Red cabbage	
Cauliflower	artichokes	Rutabagas	
Cavolo nero	Kale	Savoy cabbage	
(black kale)	Leeks	Spinach	

HERBS

Bay
Rosemary
Sage

FISH

Flatfish
Haddock
Mackerel
Mollusks
Oysters
Sea bass

MEAT

Goose

There has been much research recently into the nutritional value of organic food, with controversial findings. Plants, whether eaten directly, or by animals and poultry such as cows, sheep, pigs, and chickens which we then consume, need to have around 50 different minerals in them to provide maximum nutrition, although some of these can be in minute quantities. If plants are short of these minerals, and if they are not present in the soil, those plants tend to be less healthy and less good for us to eat.

To make up for the lack of minerals in less-rich soil, farmers feed their crops with artificial fertilizers, which consist of just three minerals: nitrogen, potassium, and phosphorus. When plants are inadequately fed, they are more susceptible to disease and marauding insects, which relish diseased plants. Farmers cannot afford to have their produce destroyed by disease and insects, so they spray it with pesticides. Plants absorb toxins both through their leaves and from the soil in which the toxins have settled. Often spraying once or twice is insufficient to keep diseases and pests at bay, so the farmers have to spray again and again, and not only the crops intended for human nutrition, but also those used for animal feed, which will in due course end up on our plates. The upshot is that our food is less nutritious in two respects—short of minerals, and potentially toxic with artificial fertilizers and pesticides.

Even though I am aware of these arguments in favor of organic food, I don't buy everything organic. But I do try to buy organic versions of the 12 so-called Dirty Dozen fruits and vegetables: peaches, apples, sweet bell peppers, celery, nectarines, strawberries, cherries, pears, grapes, spinach, lettuce, and potatoes.

We have endeavored to use ingredients in our recipes that are, on the whole, easily available. This reflects the food revolution that has been happening over the last few years. Kale, for example, was an obscure, unloved vegetable before its discovery as a "superfood." In 2013, sales of this low-calorie, high-fiber vegetable in the UK were up by 40 percent compared to the previous year. And in the US, kale sales were up 31.8 percent in 2014 over the previous year. We hope some recipes may inspire you

to try new ingredients, but plenty of others use pantry and supermarket staples, which don't require a trip to the health-food store.

I recommend doing one big first shopping to get certain essentials for the pantry and the fridge if you can afford to do so. These are ingredients that our recipes use time and time again.

Coconut oil
If you keep this in the fridge, it hardens and can be spread on toast. I mix it with olive oil as well, as a healthy alternative to olive-oil-based margarines. It is generally solid at room temperature, and when warmed up melts and can be poured, like other oils. This will depend on the time of year and how warm your kitchen is. Because it is more stable when heated than, for example, vegetable oil, it is better for frying at higher temperatures. For cakes and more precise recipes, we give liquid measures to ensure you are using the right amount. For other recipes, you can afford to be a little more relaxed. It can also be used as a body oil and as a hair treatment.

Extra-virgin olive oil
Always worth getting better-quality stuff if you can, to benefit from its health-giving properties. Cheaper basic olive oil is often treated with hexane and caustic soda, which is rather worrying. As well as using olive oil in dressings, we do cook with it at lower temperatures in some recipes, as we believe it still retains beneficial properties when heated.

Toasted sesame oil
Useful for Asian flavors, and it does have some beneficial omega-6 fatty acids, though we don't use it too often.

Active-culture yogurt
There are so many types of plain yohurt. Our recipes often call for Greek yogurt, which is much thicker, but full-fat natural yogurt works in many cases.

Spices
Ground cumin, ground coriander, cayenne pepper, paprika, Chinese five-spice powder, and turmeric are the six spices I have sitting beside my stove at all times.

Dried chili flakes
I find myself sprinkling these on almost everything. A few make a dish look decorative and you can control how spicy you want it to be. Fresh chilies are even better, of course, once you get used to the different kinds. I make a note of which works best in each recipe, because the strength can vary so much.

Cinnamon
You can buy this ground or as sticks. The sticks work out to be more expensive because you can only use them once.

Nutmeg
This is best bought whole and grated when you need it—the smell is amazing.

Nuts and seeds
I have a shelf in my kitchen with a selection of nuts and seeds ready for me to dip into whenever I feel like a snack. My favorites are walnuts, Brazil nuts, pumpkin seeds, almonds, sunflower seeds, and cashews. I have a big jar of ready-toasted nuts for sprinkling on dishes.

Spelt flour
Spelt flour was not something I ever bought before, but I find myself using it all the time now and the children don't seem to notice the difference. You can use whole wheat or other whole-grain flour if you

can't find spelt, or even more adventurous alternatives such as brown rice, quinoa, or coconut flour, all of which are gluten-free.

Maple syrup

You'll see we use this or honey as a sweetener in place of refined sugars. You need the pure, unprocessed type rather than maple-flavored syrup. No sugar, whether refined or not, should be used in excess, but the Canadians do claim that natural maple syrup has more beneficial compounds than other types of sugar. It is lower in fructose than agave nectar, and so is better for our livers. Nonetheless, don't be fooled: it still counts as sugar.

Dates

Another sweetener, and although they're high in fructose, they are rich in fiber and iron too. We don't use many of them, but they are handy for baking as they can bind ingredients together and add a toffee taste to dishes.

Garlic

A wonderful all-around ingredient for both flavor and health-giving properties. When a recipe specifies crushed garlic, try to do this by hand using a mortar and pestle, which is the best way to retain the benefits found in the allicin component of its oil. If you don't have a mortar and pestle, you can crush it with the back of a knife.

Fresh ginger

You will find it grated, sliced, or crushed in so many of our recipes and drinks.

Tahini

Buy a big jar of this and use it to make your own hummus, or a creamy vinaigrette.

Oatcakes

I always have a package of these in my pantry and use them for snacks and breakfasts. They are a type of Scottish savory whole-grain oat cracker. Go gluten-free if you want to, though I prefer the regular ones.

Miso paste

A Japanese fermented soybean paste. I often use little sachets, or buy a jar of it from the health-food store or a supermarket for Asian recipes, fish, and some dressings.

Tamari and soy sauce

I use these to add saltiness to dishes with Asian flavors. They are similar in color and flavor and both are made from fermented soybeans, but there are a number of differences between them, the main one being that soy contains wheat, while tamari doesn't. Soy is stronger and saltier, so I tend to go for tamari, which is more gentle and balancing. Always check the ingredients for MSG, which is commonly added to more processed soy sauces, and go for MSG-free versions whenever possible.

Sweeter Asian sauces

Although hoisin, sweet chili, and teriyaki sauces contain sugar, I do use them sparingly from time to time, for example as sweeteners in a savory dish. I go for the best-quality brands, which don't contain preservatives or MSG.

KITCHEN ESSENTIALS

Knives, peeler, and grater

I bought a new set of knives and a sharp grater when I first started to cook regularly. It is impossible to peel all the fruits and vegetables and indeed to cook in general without the proper tools. I use a microplane grater for zesting lemons and grating ginger, nutmeg, and even garlic.

Food processor

I bought a Magimix food processor, although a common blender should do as well. In an ideal world I would say that you need both a NutriBullet (or something similar) and a Magimix, but I had to choose one of them. The NutriBullet is fashionable right now and effective for almost everything except making nut butter, raw ice creams, and cakes. It makes smooth juices, smoothies, sauces, pesto, soups, and hummus, but it does tend to make everything the same consistency, which is its strength, of course, but means that sometimes you can lose texture in the ingredients. It is less good, however, for dry ingredients. The Magimix, on the other hand, is useful for ice creams and sorbets, and for rough-chopping nuts, herbs, and drier things in general. It has a smaller bowl too, so you can make smaller quantities, and it's great if you want to combine something rather than purée it. You can use the grater attachment to grate carrots, cauliflower, cabbage, and other vegetables, which we do throughout this book. A Magimix can last a lifetime, it's tough, and it can cut through the most frozen of bananas.

Digital weighing scales

I find these more accurate than more traditional scales for measuring small quantities. They can be reset to allow for the weight of a saucepan, mixing bowl, or spoon, and the units can be switched from grams to ounces and even to milliliters for measuring liquids. You can go for more fancy ones, or choose an inexpensive version from Bed Bath and Beyond or online for around $20—they should be reliable as long as you treat them well.

Measuring spoons and measuring cups

Measuring spoons, like teaspoons, tend to vanish in my kitchen, so I have bought myself a brand-new set. Of course, you can always use your regular cutlery—as long as you stick to the same spoon sizes throughout a recipe, you can't go too far wrong. But I am a bit nervous about recipes and find it difficult to go off-script, so I prefer to have a clear idea of what quantity a recipe calls for the first time I make it. The same applies for measuring cups, although I have been known to use a milk bottle in the past.

Nut bags

If you want to enjoy making nut milks or oat milks regularly, these do speed the process up enormously and there will be a lot less mess when you're filtering. I got mine online cheaply, and housewares stores sell them.

Veggie wash

Although I buy some organic vegetables, I don't always find that I can get what I want, plus they can be very expensive. Ergo veggie wash, a liquid that removes pesticide residues from vegetables and is safe to consume. It can be used for anything that you don't want to peel and is great for berries, which are impossible to wash one by one. You can buy it online or from health-food stores.

INDEX

Rachel Kelly
Rachel was a journalist at *The Times* for many years. Her most recent book was *Walking on Sunshine: 52 Small Steps to Happiness*. Overhauling her diet has led to a calmer, more balanced life.

Alice Mackintosh
Alice gained a first-class honors degree in nutritional therapy at the UK's Centre for Nutrition Education, following a degree in biomedical sciences at Leeds University. She runs her own clinic in London where she treats people with a wide range of conditions, including anxiety. She is cofounder of Equi London, which creates high-quality supplements designed for people who don't always find the time to eat well.

Further resources

For more details on the studies we refer to throughout the book as well as other resources, please go to our website: thehappykitchen.net.

Other sites we've found helpful include www.mind.org.uk—which includes Mind's guidelines on the relationship between mood and food. The National Health Service, too, has produced an info sheet on eating for mental well-being: www.nuh.nhs.uk/media/11284/Food%20and%20Your%20Mood.pdf.

Meanwhile, the Institute of Food, Brain and Behaviour: www.ifbb.org.uk is a helpful resource, especially on the importance of omega-3s. So, too, is the Royal Institute of Psychiatrists: www.rcpsych.ac.uk; see, for example, their section on herbal remedies and supplements, at www.rcpsych.ac.uk/healthadvice/treatmentswellbeing/complementarytherapy.aspx.

The Food Standards Agency also has a useful website—www.food.gov.uk—which looks at the evidence and research on vitamins and supplements.

Web Resources

National Institute of Mental Health
www.nimh.nih.gov/index.shtml
MentalHealth.gov
www.mentalhealth.gov/index.html
Mental Health America (MHA)
www.mentalhealthamerica.net/conditions/healthy-diet-eating-mental-health-mind
Nutrition.gov
www.nutrition.gov/dietary-supplements

Books

Gut: The inside story of our body's most underrated organ, Giulia Enders, Scribe, 2014.
Anxiety for Beginners: A personal investigation, Eleanor Morgan, Bluebird, 2016.
Anxiety and Depression: Eat your way to better health, Dale Pinnock, Quadrille Publishing, 2015.
The Diet Myth: The real science behind what we eat, Tim Spector, Weidenfeld & Nicolson, 2015.
Rise: Surviving and thriving after trauma, Sian Williams, Weidenfeld & Nicolson, 2016.

How Not to Die, Michael Greger, Flatiron Books, 2015.
Nutrition and Mental Health: A handbook, edited by Martina Watts, Pavilion Publishing and Media, 2008.
Beating Stress, Anxiety, and Depression: Groundbreaking ways to help you feel better, Professor Jane Plant and Janet Stephenson, Piatkus, 2008.
The Encyclopedia of Healing Foods, Michael Murray, Atria, 2005.
Feeling Good: The New Mood Therapy, Daniel D. Burns, Harper, 1980.
Healing Anxiety and Depression: Based on Cutting-Edge Brain Imaging Science, Daniel G. Amen, 2003.
Brain Maker: The Power of Gut Microbes to Heal and Protect Your Brain—for Life, David Perlmutter, 2015.
The Mood Cure: The 4-Step Program to Take Charge of Your Emotions—Today, Julia Ross, 2002.

Acknowledgments

I am grateful to all who loaned their culinary and nutritional expertise during the writing of this book. Lucy Maxwell was a wonderful, constant, and supportive companion in the kitchen who taught me to cook and shared her recipes and ideas. Other friends and colleagues who helped me develop my Golden Rules and recipes and shared their thoughts on what makes for a happy kitchen include Sabrina Ceol, Eliza Hoyer Millar, Tara Maxwell, Cecilia Clarke, Linda Kelly, Chloe James, Chloe Gwynne, Neville Gwynne, Dr. Nina Bailey, Dr. Carla Croft, Dr. Zofia Stanley, Dr. Safia Debar, Dr. Richard Marsh, Dr. Owen Bowden-Jones, Anna Taylor, Annabel Nourse, Raphael Rifkin-Zybutz, Emma Russell, Leo Meyer, Andrew Fergusson, and Lucien Williams. Thanks to the superb team at Short Books, Aurea Carpenter and Rebecca Nicolson and designer Georgia Vaux; and at Atria Books, Judith Curr, Peter Borland, Daniella Wexler, and Nancy Tonik. Above all, thanks to my family for coming on my Good Mood Food journey with such humor and grace.

A note to end this book

A happy kitchen is about so much more than what we eat. The people we cook for and eat with, the setting, and even the way we eat can all take us from feeling low to seeing things in a new light. Eating is one of life's greatest joys. It is no coincidence that many of our most important conversations take place over the kitchen table. Being anxious can take away part of our identities, but I have found that following my Golden Rules and eating our recipes has helped me become a calmer, happier person. We would love to hear about your experience of a happy diet, so please share any ways in which you have created your own joyous recipes and kitchen. We would be delighted if you tagged us in any Good Mood Food recipe creations on social media using the hashtag #happykitchenbook. For more inspiration, pictures, and nutritional news, our website is thehappykitchen.net and our Instagram account is @happykitchenbook. Below are details of how to get in touch. Please do!

Rachel
info@rachel-kelly.net
Twitter: @RachelKellyNet
www.rachel-kelly.net

Alice
Twitter @AliceMackintosh
Instagram: @alicemack
www.alicemackintosh.com

CUT-OUT
GOOD MOOD
FOOD INDEX

A handy guide to stick on your fridge

FAB MOOD FOODS

Arugula
Avocados
Blueberries
Chamomile tea
Cavolo nero (black kale)
Crabmeat (brown & white)
Eggs
Flaxseed—in moderation
Goji berries
Green tea
Hempseed—in moderation
Kale
Kefir
Kimchi
Lentils (all types)
Mackerel
Marmite
Mushrooms
Natural organic yogurt
Oatcakes
Oats
Pecans—in moderation
Pumpkin seeds—in moderation
Quinoa
Raw cacao powder
Saffron
Salmon
Sauerkraut
Shrimp
Spinach
Sweet potatoes
Tuna
Turmeric
Walnuts—in moderation
Watercress

VERY GOOD MOOD FOODS

Almonds—in moderation
Bananas
Beets
Brazil nuts
Broccoli
Brown rice
Butternut squash
Cherries
Chia seeds—in moderation
Chicken (with skin)
Chickpeas
Chilies
Cinnamon
Dark chocolate, minimum 70% cocoa solids—in moderation
Edamame
Olive oil
Peppers (all colors)
Raspberries
Red cabbage
Rye bread
Seaweed
Strawberries

GOOD MOOD FOODS

Beef (lean cuts)
Buckwheat flour
Canned fish—refer to our advice on types and quantities in the Golden Rules
Cashews—in moderation
Cayenne pepper
Chicken livers
Cilantro, mint, parsley, and other fresh herbs
Coconut (fresh)
Eggplant
Fava beans
Ginger
Goat cheese
Granola (homemade)
Lemons
Miso
Peas
Spelt pasta
Sugar snap peas
Tahini
Tomatoes (canned or fresh)
Whole-grain flour (or spelt)
Whole-grain pasta
Zucchini

TREATS

Alcohol
Black tea—2 cups a day is adequate; don't add sugar
Butter
Cheesy pasta dishes
Coffee—2 cups a day is adequate; no added sugar
Cookies
Cream
Desserts
Dried fruit
Fruit juices
Fruit smoothies (store bought)
Maple syrup
Mayonnaise and other creamy dressings
Milk and white chocolate
Packaged sandwiches
Peanuts
Pork (especially fatty cuts)
Potato chips and other similar snacks
Sauces in jars (pasta sauce and similar)
Sausages and bacon
Sunflower oil
White bread and bread products (including bagels, croissants, white crackers)
White refined grains (pasta, rice, couscous)

LOW MOOD FOODS

Canned soups—some are fine but check ingredients carefully
Cereal bars
Diet drinks
Energy drinks
Food colorings
Low-fat "diet" snacks
Margarine
MSG (and other food additives)
Pastries, sweet baked goods (doughnuts, croissants, cookies)
Prepared meals
Refined white sugar
Sweetened and processed breakfast cereals—check the ingredients for added sugar and avoid anything processed, choosing whole grains where possible. Some less-processed cereals are fine, often fortified and a source of iron and B vitamins
Sweet fizzy drinks
Take-out meals—be careful. There are some pretty healthy ones now, though, which take care to use fresh ingredients
Wafer-thin ham and similar processed meats